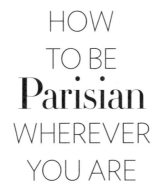

HOW TO BE Parisian WHEREVER YOU ARE

Love, Style, and Bad Habits

ANNE BEREST

AUDREY DIWAN

CAROLINE DE MAIGRET

SOPHIE MAS

DOUBLEDAY NEW YORK LONDON TORONTO SYDNEY AUCKLAND

All rights reserved. Published in the United States by Doubleday, a division of Random House LLC, New York, and in Canada by Random House of Canada Limited, Toronto, Penguin Random House companies.

This is a translation of the unpublished French manuscript copyright © Anne Berest, Audrey Diwan, Caroline de Maigret, and Sophie Mas

www.doubleday.com

DOUBLEDAY and the portrayal of an anchor with a dolphin are registered trademarks of Random House LLC.

LIBRARY OF CONGRESS CATALOGING-IN-PUBLICATION DATA
Berest, Anne, 1979–
How to be Parisian wherever you are : love, style, and bad habits/
Anne Berest, Audrey Diwan, Caroline de Maigret, Sophie Mas.
— First edition.
pages cm
ISBN: 978-0-385-53865-7 (hardback)
ISBN: 978-0-385-53866-4 (eBook)
1. Women—France—Paris—Social life and customs.
2. French—Social life and customs. 3. Fashion—France—
Paris. 4. Man-woman relationships—France—Paris. 5. Paris
(France)—Civilization—21st century. I. Title.
HQ1613.B43 2014
305.40944'361—dc23
2014012863

MANUFACTURED IN THE UNITED STATES OF AMERICA

1   3   5   7   9   10   8   6   4   2

First Edition

HOW TO BE **Parisian** WHEREVER YOU ARE

A story should have a beginning, a middle and an end, but not necessarily in that order.

—JEAN-LUC GODARD

CONTENTS

2. Own Your Bad Habits

3. Cultivate Your Allure

4. Dare to Love

5. Parisian Tips

HOW

TO BE

Parisian

WHEREVER

YOU ARE

INTRODUCTION

The truth is out: Parisiennes aren't privy to a secret "skinny" gene, they aren't always easy to be with, and aren't all perfect mothers. In fact, they are very imperfect, vague, unreliable, and full of paradoxes. But they can also be funny, attentive, curious, and ironic, and they know how to enjoy life.

We are four Parisian women who have been friends for ages. We are very different in many ways but always agree about the important things. We've spent countless long nights laughing with each other and sharing that typically French enthusiasm for transforming life into fiction. As you'll discover, Parisian women spend an inordinate amount of energy trying to spin every episode of their existence into a very good story.

Our aim here is to give you an insight into the quintessentially Parisian art of being a woman. We're methodical and yet shambolic, proud and yet self-deprecating, loyal and yet unfaithful. We'll point out our attitude, nonchalance, our low-key style, what we are like in love, and how we choose to spend our days and nights. We hope that the following pages will dispel the mystery.

I

GET THE BASICS

APHORISMS

**To be read out loud every night before going to bed.
Even when inebriated:**

Don't be afraid of aging. As the saying goes, don't be afraid of anything
but fear itself. * **Find "your" perfume before you turn thirty.
Wear it for the next thirty years.** * No one should ever see your
gums when you talk or laugh. * **If you own only one sweater, make
sure it's cashmere.** * Wear a black bra under your white blouse, like
two notes on a sheet of music. * **One must live with the opposite
sex, not against them. Except when making love.** * Be
unfaithful: cheat on your perfume, but only on cold days. * **Go
to the theater, to museums, and to concerts as often as
possible: it gives you a healthy glow.** * Be aware of your qualities
and your faults. Cultivate them in private but don't obsess. * **Make
it look easy. Everything you do should seem effortless and
graceful.** * Not too much makeup, too many colors, too many
accessories . . . * **Take a deep breath and keep it simple.** * Your
look should always have one thing left undone—the devil is in the
details. * **Be your own knight in shining armor.** * Cut your own
hair or ask your sister to do it for you. Of course you know celebrity
hairdressers, but only as friends. * **Always be fuckable: when
standing in line at the bakery on a Sunday morning, buying
champagne in the middle of the night, or even picking the kids
up from school. You never know.** * Either go all gray or no gray
hair. Salt and pepper is for the table. * **Fashion rules the world and
Parisians rule fashion. Fine, it may not be true. But the world
still needs fairy tales.**

The Parisienne as Seen by a Parisian Man

Who could I ask for the perfect definition of the Parisienne?

I'd asked myself that question countless times, until I had an epiphany.

Of course: ask him. That guy in the kitchen who happens to share my life.

He was surprised by my question, and muttered a few words to himself.

I watched him, exasperated.

Doesn't he have anything original to say, something beyond the usual clichés about our incredible style and iconic perfume?

"Wait, you're being serious? We're really talking about this?" he asked, before leaning against the sink. And then he started, and didn't stop. As though reciting a prayer learned by heart, one he knew with his eyes closed.

First off, he says, the Parisienne is never satisfied. Here's proof: I'm telling you how gorgeous you are and it's never enough.

The Parisienne thinks she's a role model. She can fill blogs and books with life advice. In fact, she *loves* being asked what she thinks. And of course that makes sense because she's already done everything. Seen everything. She knows it all.

For example, the Parisienne will always refer you to her doctor—he's a genius. Her dentist—he's an artist, his work is like a fine jeweler's. And her gynecologist—well, of course, Catherine Deneuve goes to him, too. The Parisienne, shamelessly snobbish, is *such* a snob that she's perfectly comfortable letting everyone know it. What's wrong with that? The Parisienne is arrogant.

Her thing is art, culture, and politics. She cultivates herself the same way she cares for her radishes growing on the balcony—that is, with love. Watering can in hand, she'll tell you how the last film to win the Palme d'Or is rotten tomatoes. But she probably hasn't even seen it. The Parisienne already knows what she must think: the opposite of what you think, no matter what.

The Parisienne is always late. Unlike you, she has important things to do, she's a busy woman. She'll never wear makeup on a date. Naturally, her inner beauty needs no artifice. On the other hand, she won't hesitate to wear lipstick to the bakery on Sunday morning, because what if she runs into someone she knows?

Her paranoia verges on megalomania. If her unquenchable thirst for subjects of dismay were used to solve equations, she'd get the Nobel Prize in mathematics every year.

Watch out if she says your new boyfriend is "so original." For her, "original" is not a compliment.

She never crosses the street where she's supposed to; she claims it's her rebellious side. People who wait in lines stress her out.

She doesn't always say thank you, doesn't always say hi, but will complain about the rudeness of Parisian waiters.

She's outspoken and can swear like a sailor. She's horrified when people politely say *"Bon appétit!"* Poor taste is worse than poor diplomacy.

She always wears her sunglasses, even when it rains. But she despises movie stars who hide behind them.

In a nutshell (and, trust me, I know her well), I'd say the Parisienne is completely *cuckoo*!

YOU
WON'T FIND IN
HER CLOSET

* Three-inch heels. Why live life halfway?

* Logos. You are not a billboard.

* Nylon, polyester, viscose, and vinyl will make you sweaty, smelly, and shiny.

* Sweatpants. No man should ever see you in those. Except your gym teacher—and even then. Leggings are tolerated.

* Blingy jeans with embroidery and holes in them. They belong to Bollywood.

* UGG boots. Enough said.

* A skimpy top. Because you're not fifteen anymore.

* A fake designer bag. Like fake breasts, you can't fix your insecurities through forgery.

    Truth be told, if the Parisienne could wear just a Burberry trench and nothing underneath, she would be in heaven.

The Most Famous Parisiennes Are Foreigners

Yes, the Parisienne often comes from somewhere else. She wasn't born in Paris, but she's reborn there.

MARIE ANTOINETTE

Marie Antoinette was Austrian. When she arrived in France to marry Louis XVI and become queen, she was just fourteen years old. A figure of frivolity, she was the first to spark our obsession with fashion. She fell in love with a man who wasn't her husband, and she dreamed of taking to the stage, or of being a shepherdess. She invented her own life.

JOSEPHINE BAKER

Born in St. Louis, Missouri, Josephine didn't merely adopt French nationality she embraced the heart and soul of the country as well, and even joined the French Resistance during World War II. She became one of the biggest Parisian stars with her cabarets at the Folies Bergère, which took Paris by storm. Liberal and avant-garde, Baker exuded sensuality and intelligence; she became phenomenally success-ful thanks to her singing "I have two loves . . . my country and Paris."

ROMY SCHNEIDER

In Paris, the lead actress in *Sissi—The Young Empress* discovered the pleasures of sleepless nights, nonconformity, and insouciance. In the sixties and

the seventies, this young woman from Vienna instantly captured the hearts of the French, who admired her charm, her kindness, and her air of fragility. She quickly became a model of femininity for all Parisiennes.

JANE BIRKIN

Jane Birkin, the British actress and singer who became the most Parisian of them all, sang the unforgettable 1969 song *"Je t'aime . . . moi non plus"* with Serge Gainsbourg, and among her many films were *Blow-up* and *Don Juan (Or If Don Juan Were a Woman)*, with Brigitte Bardot. The French love her British accent, and she is now part of their national heritage. Her daughters, Charlotte Gainsbourg and Lou Doillon, have followed in her footsteps and continue to teach us lessons about a style that is timeless: used jeans, a trench, and sneakers.

1:00 P.M.

First Date at the Café de Flore

She picks up the menu. Each time, the same thought crosses her mind: in her hands, this is more of a geographical map than a restaurant menu. It is an intimate, chaotic, and complicated path through the jungle of her culinary neuroses. And she can't fight the looming idea that she will have to battle her way, keeping up appearances, without stumbling and, especially, without looking like she's asking herself too many questions.

Smoked salmon

No, wrong choice. She'll just end up using the salmon as a pretext for eating all the blinis and crème fraîche. Her greed could end up on her hips.

Does this man sitting across from her realize how difficult it is to be a woman in this city? Probably not. And she doesn't want to judge him too quickly. She continues her stroll through the list of appetizers; she's on home ground.

Haricots verts salad

The problem with a first date is that her every gesture will take on a particular meaning. He's watching her as if he's filming her, recording her movements forever: the way in which she loses her phone in her large handbag, and in turn loses herself while searching for it, and that message on her voice mail she can't help listening to in front of him. He is analyzing her. Disorganized, a tad nervous, compulsively sociable. Maybe he senses the difficulty she is having making up her mind. But she doesn't want to reveal too soon the war she is waging in silence. Perhaps one day, later on, he will find out that she weighs herself every morning, but for now, he must believe that her figure is simply nature's gift. Better to choose a real dish, giving him the hackneyed image of a bon vivant and letting him believe that this is her approach to all the great pleasures of life.

Warm duck confit

Her finger, somewhat nervously, scrolls down several lines on this damned menu. She cannot find an honorable way out, and she's mad at herself. For here, on the terrace, time is running out, passersby brush against her, the waiter is coming over, and she knows she will have to come to a decision. And so she figures she will brave the danger with an act of courage. She will choose something original:

"Welsh rarebit," she says.

She is adventurous and proud to show it. She is drawing a clear distinction between herself and other girls. She feels she is showing a certain audacity, putting it on the table, as if it were a trophy. She reads out the foreign words so casually you'd think she'd done it a hundred times before. She hopes that the waiter will not pick up on her accent, betraying her little show. The man opposite her looks up, surprised, and she savors the effect it has on him. Of course, she has no idea what she's just ordered. On the menu, in small print, it says: "a specialty made from cheddar, beer, and toast." Inwardly she smiles: inedible. No matter, she will talk enough for him not to notice that she's ignoring her plate. The waiter then turns to the man.

"I'll have the same, please," he says.

And in a flash, the whole scene crumbles. Oh no, a sheep, a follower, what a bore. Suddenly, her eyes are opened, and she realizes that his conversation has been peppered with banalities for the past half hour. She now knows she'll eat two bites, then find a reason to leave before the hour is up. And she will never see him again. *Adieu.*

A SERIOUS TEXT ABOUT HUMOR

There is nothing more difficult than explaining humor. Nothing more boring, either. Humor is very particular, it has its own color and culture.

If you had to describe Parisian humor, you could say it is both cold and sarcastic. You would find it is prone to joyous despair, likes paradox, and entertains a rather disillusioned idea of life and love (coupled with the certainty that they are both nevertheless worth it). Favorite humorous topics include the relationship between men and women, often from a sexual point of view, as well as the balance of power between the two. It is irreverent and touches on taboos without being completely scathing. It will not lapse into "jokes" per se, but it is omnipresent and used whenever, wherever possible. It is a snobbish humor, often with a bit of self-deprecation. Indeed, playing up the least flattering anecdotes about yourself is considered good taste. Amusing your friends by recounting your setbacks or embarrassments is a genuine sport, practiced by Parisians who otherwise do none, because laughing at yourself is better for your health than crying (especially in the absence of any other sport).

"Will you be my first wife?"

—SACHA GUITRY

PARISIAN PUZZLE-**WINTER**

Moleskin notebook	Rooftops by night	Morning mist	Clouds over the Pont Neuf	A thick shawl	A bistro table
A run in your tights	Slate roofs	Hints of eau de cologne	Frozen statues	Chairs in the Luxembourg Gardens	A new diary
The Seine overflowing	A pretty silk scarf	*Marrons glacés*	A soft sweater	Sometimes it snows	A renovated faça
Place des Victoires	Old Persian rugs	Two hot chocolates	Chipped nail polish	It's always raining	Lampposts
A felt hat	Slippery sidewalks	Chimney tops	Parquet floors	Sandalwood candle	Wrought iron
Rose-flavored *macaron*	Seats in a movie theater	Empty park benches	A rock song	*Le Monde*	Montmartre is co
Sunday in bed	Out the window	The Louvre	A mean Yorkshire terrier	A thermal T-shirt	Men's ties
Veal blanquette	Oysters	A glass of Bordeaux	Reading under the covers	Rue de Paradis	A nice hot bath

PARISIAN PUZZLE–**SUMMER**

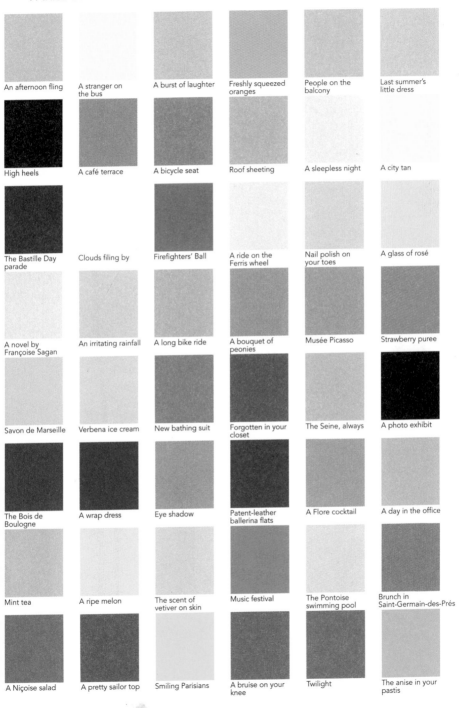

An afternoon fling

A stranger on the bus

A burst of laughter

Freshly squeezed oranges

People on the balcony

Last summer's little dress

High heels

A café terrace

A bicycle seat

Roof sheeting

A sleepless night

A city tan

The Bastille Day parade

Clouds filing by

Firefighters' Ball

A ride on the Ferris wheel

Nail polish on your toes

A glass of rosé

A novel by Françoise Sagan

An irritating rainfall

A long bike ride

A bouquet of peonies

Musée Picasso

Strawberry puree

Savon de Marseille

Verbena ice cream

New bathing suit

Forgotten in your closet

The Seine, always

A photo exhibit

The Bois de Boulogne

A wrap dress

Eye shadow

Patent-leather ballerina flats

A Flore cocktail

A day in the office

Mint tea

A ripe melon

The scent of vetiver on skin

Music festival

The Pontoise swimming pool

Brunch in Saint-Germain-des-Prés

A Niçoise salad

A pretty sailor top

Smiling Parisians

A bruise on your knee

Twilight

The anise in your pastis

A
KIND
OF
BLUE

She's Parisian, which is to say she's melancholy. Her mood responds to the changing colors of her city. She can feel a sudden surge of sorrow or even hope for no reason at all. In the blink of an eye, all those lost memories and smells come flooding back, reminding her of loved ones who are no longer there. And time passing by.

It never lasts very long, but this particular mood takes her away from the world for a few instants and gives her that absent-minded, absorbed look she has every now and again.

She's sitting alone in a restaurant. She's not waiting for anyone, her book is on the table as she gazes so far off into the distance that her surroundings are a blur and she doesn't even hear the laughter around her.

From a taxi she watches silently as neighborhoods unfold before her and happy people hurry by. She sighs and asks the driver to turn up the music to help drown out her thoughts.

In the early morning she's the lone figure walking out of the Métro as the crowds rush in. Her hair is a bit disheveled and she still is wearing her jewelry from last night. As she heads home her heart is breaking, but no one will ever know why.

Someone is talking to her, but she's not listening . . . All she can think about is the faint smell of burning candles that carries her back to a long-lost part of her childhood.

During the summer months she is particularly sensitive as the daylight begins to fade. She feels as though the world's troubles are flowing through her. She doesn't feel like talking, and stays in her bedroom until the sun has set.

A Mother
with Flaws

et's be honest: the Parisienne is a selfish woman. A loving mother, yes, but nonetheless incapable of forgetting herself completely. In Paris you won't find many *mater dolorosa*, sacrificial women whose lives revolve around cooking shepherd's pie for their numerous progeny. The Parisienne does not stop existing the day she has a child. She does not give up her somewhat adolescent lifestyle, her nights out with friends, her parties, or her mornings-after feeling worse for wear. Indeed, she doesn't give up anything, because she also embraces her role as a mother. She wants to be there to educate her child, to watch him grow up, to pass on her values, her culture, her philosophy. **And what happens in the life of a woman who refuses to give up anything? Disorder—and lots of it.** A disorder so normal it may even become, through repetition, a new form of order. And this is perhaps the guiding principle of a Parisian mother's education system. Her child is not king, because he is a satellite to her own life. At the same time, her child is omnipresent because this satellite follows his mother everywhere, and together they share valuable moments. He might join her at a lunch, accompany her to a boutique, end up at a concert or a cocktail party, where he will fall asleep on a sofa as she watches over him with equal amounts of guilt and tenderness. Her child also goes to school and to the park, and plays tennis, joins sports teams, or takes English lessons. Sometimes even all at once. These moments between two ages, these moments of complicity that would normally be forbidden, become regular exceptions, fun detours to throw the child's timetable off track. And in general, neither is complaining. Later on, they will both cherish these fleeting images, fragments of conversation gleaned here and there, the vestiges of the adult world he will have caught a glimpse of, helping him to form a joyful image of what awaits him one day. According to the Parisienne, this *joie de vivre* is the best way of inspiring children to grow up. And also the best way for mothers to never miss the lives they led before they had children.

How to Answer the Telephone
When He Finally Calls

The telephone rings, she answers.

The Parisienne lets the phone ring. (She's not waiting by the phone.)
She feigns surprise upon hearing his voice. (She wasn't expecting
his call.)
She asks if she can call him back in five minutes. (She's in the middle
of something.)
The thing is, she's not alone . . . (*Et oui:* you should never have kept
her waiting.)

VIRTUES OF THE SIGNATURE ITEM

The Parisienne's signature item is that vital detail that brings her outfit together, from head to toe.

You don't have to spend a decade's worth of salary on your wardrobe, or flaunt designer brands the whole time. All you need is one signature item: the one you wear when you need to feel strong.

Not every Parisienne has a grandmother who opens her armoire and exclaims, "Take whatever you want, my dear!" Far from it. But no matter. The Parisienne is a bargain hunter, whether at the flea market or on eBay. This is where she finds the perfect item or accessory that she'll wear for the rest of her life.

Whether it's a trench coat, a pair of stilettos, or a leather purse, the item is precious. Take excellent care of it but, most important, wear it—with jeans, ballet flats, or a cargo jacket. Make sure to keep the rest of your outfit simple, so as to avoid looking like a Christmas tree.

Remember: your signature item is a piece that looks amazing on you; it drapes perfectly around your shoulders, it makes your every gesture seem effortless and graceful. The fabric is flawless and the finishes are perfect—but it should never be gaudy or loud.

A signature item never gives itself away. It's timeless. It transcends fashion. It is discreet—the letters of the alphabet (two Cs, a large D; the combination of Y, S, and L) belong on an ophthalmologist's chart. For the Parisienne, luxury should never be spelled out.

The signature item is a gift that a woman gives herself depending on her age, her taste, and the size of her purse. It is a symbol of independence and freedom, which states, "I bought this for myself. I earned it and it makes me happy."

The signature item is an attitude. It is the gun in your holster that makes you feel well dressed and invincible.

Au Naturel

It is almost impossible to resolve the great mystery of what is natural. Because, in fact, nothing is natural. Parisiennes will have you believe that they are born with perfect skin and delightfully messy hair. That from the cradle onward they exude a scent worthy of Chanel Nº5. That these "natural" attributes are a heritage that cannot be explained.

They are all lying.

Au naturel is the fruit of hard labor, meticulously passed down from generation to generation. What follows is a series of unusual tips that could be summed up as follows: how to take care of yourself while giving the impression that you don't take care of yourself. It is the art of beauty—the Parisian way.

ALL YOU NEED TO KNOW ABOUT HAIR

One of the Parisienne's most distinctive features is her head of hair. There are several characteristics that make it easy to identify. Her hairstyle is never "immaculate" and it's rare that she goes for a blowout. She cultivates, depending on her age, a type of capillary blur, to varying degrees of tidiness. But make no mistake, this is a very carefully organized chaos.

HOW: Do not dye your hair, or if you do, only in your original color to highlight it, or to hide any gray. This rule is more or less followed by everyone: you keep the color Mother Nature chose for you.

Do not dry your hair with a hair dryer (in fact, you might as well throw your hair dryer away) but instead use two much more environmentally friendly resources: fresh air in summer and a towel in winter. Whenever possible, wash your hair in the evening rather than in the morning, so as not to leave the house with wet hair.

Falling asleep with damp hair will give it a more interesting shape when you wake up. It's not worth washing your hair every day, as it's usually on the following day (or even the day after that, depending on the texture of your hair) that your hair gains a certain weight that in turn gives it the right volume when tied up in a bun.

There's no point in accessorizing your hair: avoid hair clips or headbands if you're over eighteen, but also hair jewelry or any other kind of decorative accessory.

And as your face gets messier with age, your hair can get neater, for balance.

Bless that magical time in summer when your hair, with some sea water and sunshine, becomes simply perfect: a little bit rough, a little bit lighter, and a little bit salty.

And, of course, a touch of perfume on your hair, behind your ear, or on the nape of your neck, never did anyone any harm . . .

ON PLASTIC SURGERY

Parisiennes do not have plastic surgery, because they believe you need to know how to accept the body your mother created with such attention and care. And not only accept it, but enhance it through a fastidious and passionate regime of self-awareness. Of course, this is what they'll have you—as well as their men—believe. But it's not true.

Until recently, plastic surgery in France was considered to be the symptom of two worrying problems: futile obsessions and manic depression. Things have evolved and now Parisiennes do have work done on their bodies and faces. But, as always, they do so their own way, that is to say they stick to certain rules. It's all about moderation.

HOW: First choose one part to focus on, one single operation. The one thing that bothers you the most. Either your nose or the area around your mouth, your breasts, or your tummy . . . Next, put off for as long as possible the age at which you first have work done. In France it is rare to find a thirty-five-year-old who has had plastic surgery. Generally, the fight begins in your forties, often with the help of hyaluronic acid or Botox (you should resort to the latter not more than once a year, or else you run the risk of it becoming visible). Having waited patiently, thanks to these preliminary procedures, the first small lifts are contemplated after the age of fifty: your eyelids, the bags under your eyes, or the wrinkles around your mouth. Then, at the age of sixty, you can think about maybe getting a "mini-lift."

Surgery is not, as in certain countries, an external symbol of wealth. A measure of its success is that it is undetectable. Indeed, in Paris, you don't talk about it, you don't tell people. The main thing is to avoid any operation that distorts or that might turn a woman into a statue or a doll.

ON SKIN

Skin should look natural. Freckles can appear in spring along with the first rays of sunshine. Sometimes your cheekbones blush when you lie, and your whole face flushes when you are intimidated. You must not stifle the stories behind the natural coloring of your skin. For this reason, it must be shown, revealed, exposed.

HOW: Frenchwomen avoid using foundation, which merely serves as a shroud and therefore trivializes.

There is a whole range of invisible artifices that can be used instead. Invisible and yet convincing—it is all about the varnish. In the same way as painters would "prepare" their canvas before adding any color (these preparations were kept secret and their recipe would disappear with the artist at his death), the skin of your face must be treated as a canvas.

Start with a moisturizer to smooth your skin, which professionals swear by. Then hide any imperfections (bags under your eyes, the sides of your nose, pimples) with concealers (such as Yves Saint Laurent's Touche Éclat) or a BB cream. If you really can't live without your foundation, then mix it with a touch of moisturizer to mute its effect. And a few strokes of mascara (Hypnôse by Lancôme)—be generous on your top and bottom lashes, to accentuate your look and disguise any bags under your eyes—and bright red lipstick (Dior Addict) will not go amiss for a night out.

LOOK AFTER YOUR EXTREMITIES

Even if the Parisienne can come across as a little nonchalant, she nevertheless respects the universal principles of femininity: well-cared-for hands and feet. What does this entail? Short, clean nails, sometimes worn with nail polish—but not always. Simplicity is key. In fact, the French manicure is something of an enigma: It is the exact opposite of French chic. The Parisienne does not understand the point of it and never wears it. It would be an overt admission that she's spent time working on her sophistication.

Despite all these routines, the Parisienne retains her little imperfections, cherishes them even (the gap in her smile or her slightly crooked tooth, her prominent eyebrows or strong nose): these are the signs of a certain strength of character and allow her to feel beautiful without being perfect.

PUBLIC PRIVACY

A Parisienne always has a good reason to be sitting on a bench

When she has time to kill because she doesn't want to show up early for a meeting that she has arrived for too soon.

When she has to rummage around in her bag to find her phone, then her car keys, then the remote for the parking lot, and then her house keys—and after all this, she's so exhausted that she doesn't even want to go home anymore.

When she is walking out for good and slams the door behind her to show she means business, and then realizes she has no idea where to go.

When she wants to kiss a man before deciding whether she should invite him up or let a lousy kiss be the last.

When she has sprinted a hundred yards for a bus but still missed it, and needs to catch her breath after this unexpected burst of physical activity.

When she has to make a phone call that no one at home should be privy to.

When she wants to read a book and to be seen reading a book.

When she wants to imagine what it will be like to be an old woman in Paris one day, talking to the pigeons for lack of better company.

Faux Pas

Every tribe has its rules, rituals, and customs that the rest of the world struggles to understand. The Parisienne is particularly strict about her set of codes. These faux pas, whether they be intellectual or sartorial, are to be avoided at all costs, lest you be considered a *plouc* (see Fifteen Words You Need).

Asking someone at a party what they do for a living. ✳ **Even worse, asking them how much money they make.** ✳ Having a wedding photo on display in your living room. ✳ **Matching your purse to your outfit.** ✳ Overdoing it on the teeth whitening. ✳ **Overplucking your eyebrows.** ✳ Being "friends" with your children. ✳ **Flaunting your money or being a cheapskate.** ✳ Using "I've had one too many" as an excuse for inappropriate behavior. ✳ **Having lip augmentation. It makes you look like a duck.** ✳ Trying too hard with your appearance. Wearing too much makeup. ✳ **Fishing for compliments.** ✳ Using corporate jargon, even if it's a common phrase: "the DNA of the company," "I can pencil you in . . ." ✳ **Having more than two different colors in your hair.** ✳ Taking yourself too seriously.

Safety Kit

Because You Never Know

_OF COURSE I'M **DYING** TO SEE HIM AGAIN.

_DID YOU GIVE HIM YOUR **NUM83R?**

_No when I left I just said:

"*We'll meet again...*"

What ?

TRUST ME:
IF A MAN WANTS **YOU**
HE'LL FIND **YOU**

BUT YOU DIDN'T
GIVE HIM
YOUR
NAME!

2

OWN YOUR BAD HABITS

YES.
BUT NO.
BUT YES.

* She says hello to everyone **but wants to talk to no one.**

* She eats a four-cheese pizza **but puts Stevia in her coffee.**

* She buys very expensive shoes **but never polishes them.**

* She behaves insufferably **and is flabbergasted when she gets dumped.**

* She goes to great lengths for a pedicure **but wears mismatched underwear.**

* She smokes like a chimney on the way to the countryside **to get some fresh air.**

* She drinks vodka in the evening **and green tea in the morning.**

* She doesn't believe in God **but prays for help whenever she's in trouble.**

* She's an environmentalist **but sometimes takes her scooter to buy a baguette.**

* She's a feminist **but watches porn.**

* She's capable of moving mountains **but is in constant need of reassurance.**

* She's aware that her flaws mess with her life.
  But changing is too much work.

How to Make Him Think You Have a Lover

Select from the following options:

* Have flowers delivered to yourself and then thank your boyfriend for the thoughtful gesture.

* Save your sister's number under the name Paul H.

* Appear lost in thought: sit by a window and stare into space.

* Cry from time to time for no reason.

* Don't answer his calls; but send him gushing texts.

* Shower frequently. Spend extra time in the bathroom.

* Buy yourself some new lingerie or take up smoking again.

HER
OWN
HIGHWAY
CODE

When it comes to driving, there's only one rule the Parisienne follows: may the best driver win.

Sometimes she'll cut off a male driver, for the sake of gender equality, to prove that she, too, has balls.

Behind the wheel she becomes fluent in sign language and occasionally gives the finger to show her frustration.

She never wastes time looking for an actual parking spot. Instead, she leaves her car wherever she wants and acts like there's valet parking, but feels persecuted whenever she gets a ticket.

Whenever she gets pulled over, the Parisienne starts to cry, before even handing over her license and registration.

Most of the time, the officer lets her go and is willing to overlook her misdemeanor. He is the only kind of man on whom her tears seem to work.

When the officer is a woman, tears are pointless. So the Parisienne resorts to shouting and ends up with a handful of points on her license. She curses her misfortune in having been caught by a woman, but feels no remorse for driving in the bus lane.

She likes taking crafty detours and side roads to avoid traffic jams. Often she wastes more time than she saves, but it's her way of feeling like she's mastered the city.

Cyclists drive her crazy. Not only do they make her feel guilty about polluting the planet, but also for not going to the gym more often and working on her thighs.

She's already had sex in a tiny car, so she knows that you always hit your knee on the hand brake in the heat of the moment. But that won't stop her from doing it again.

When she's running late, she does her makeup in the car. A rearview mirror is still a mirror.

She sometimes sings along to oldies at the top of her lungs, songs she wouldn't be caught dead singing along to beyond the secret confines of her car.

The dashboard is an extension of her handbag—a notorious mess strewn with anything and everything: a crime novel, an old pay stub, a pack of gum, a phone charger, a wilted rose. As an ensemble, they are part diary and part psychedelic art, on view for the world to admire.

The Parisienne doesn't stop driving when her gas light goes on. Instead she prefers to play her own form of Russian roulette: Will she make it, or won't she?

KISS AND PLAY

W hen it comes to kissing, the Parisienne does it the same way she does everything else: with cinematic flair. Preferably, all kissing should take place in the middle of the street. The city is after all her stage and she treats each kiss like a once-in-a-lifetime performance. She wants to be unforgettable—both to the man clinging to her lips and to the people passing by. Like any good actress, she immerses herself completely in the role and almost expects a round of applause when the curtain falls at the end of her scene. *Breathless,* of course.

Hosting a Dinner Party

Behind the Scenes

Like Coco Chanel, do your utmost to avoid dinners with more than six guests around the table. In Paris, an evening often starts with a bottle of champagne, served with ice. If possible, get the conversation flowing with a controversial political statement.

— As a matter of fact, we're witnessing a shift in the class struggle. It's no longer workers against employers; it's about immigration. And at the end of the day, it's the poor against the poor.

— Capitalism has succeeded in its aim of making sure that the workers are no longer battling against those above them, but instead, those below them. Marx was right all along.

— You have no idea what you're talking about—you're just throwing around notions you don't actually understand.

— Okay then, explain to me the difference between the right and the left.

— It's very simple! For the right, if the individual thrives, so does society. For the left, if society thrives, so does the individual.

Once the guests have stopped arguing and the conversation is beginning to wear thin, to avoid veering toward the topic of children, the hostess should then suggest that everyone take their seats at the dinner table.

She hasn't prepared an appetizer and goes straight to the main course. After all, it's not as though she didn't have other things to do with her day.

The trick lies not in being a gourmet chef, but rather mastering a couple of recipes perfectly. One of them should be easy so that you can rustle it up at the last minute. The other should be very complicated, to wow your friends.

The portions should be generous and the table should look pretty. Don't forget the flowers. Above all, the cook should never appear stressed out—everything must look *effortless*.

LEMON CHICKEN

INGREDIENTS

1 large chicken, ready to roast
2 lemons
1 tin of small candied lemons
Cinnamon, a few pinches to taste
1 onion, to taste (optional)
2 tablespoons soy sauce

Serves 4–5
Prep time: 15 minutes
Cooking time: 2 hours

- Preheat the oven to 350°F.

- Place the chicken in a cast-iron pot.

- Zest the lemons (if they are not organic, wash them with soap beforehand).

- Pour the juice of one lemon over the chicken.

- Cut the candied lemons in half, adding them and their juices into the pot, along with the lemon zest.

- Peel the second lemon, and stuff the chicken with it.

- Rub the cinnamon onto the chicken, which will give it a nice crispy, brown skin (without having to use any oil).

- Add the onion, finely sliced, if using.

- Cook for 2 hours in the oven.

- After 1 hour, turn the chicken over to make sure it cooks on both sides.

- After another 45 minutes, turn it back over and baste it with the soy sauce.

  NOTE: Don't add salt, as the juices of the candied lemons already contain plenty.

While your guests are savoring your chicken, redirect the conversation around to a Parisian's second favorite dinner topic: sex.

— For example, I realized I love it when he calls me "you little slut" in bed. "Bitch," on the other hand, really gets on my nerves.

— Oh, "bitch" is fine; it just depends on the context. Like "little bitch" is completely different from "bitch" on its own. "Naughty bitch" is quite sweet too, I like it.

The Parisienne also has an old family recipe up her sleeve, passed down from generation to generation, which requires much more preparation, often a couple of days in advance. (Shop two days beforehand, begin cooking the day before.) The most important thing is to always say, "Oh no, it's nothing special, just something I threw together," and to never disclose your recipes or where you bought your ingredients.

POT-AU-FEU

Prepare this the day before in order to leave time to degrease.

INGREDIENTS
Sea salt and freshly ground pepper
3 pounds of beef (preferably cheek, but if you can't find it, use shank or brisket)

1 good-sized carrot per person, plus one for the stock, peeled and
    cut into quarters

1 large onion, studded with cloves

1 garlic clove, with the skin left on

1 long celery stalk, cut into quarters

1 bouquet garni, including parsley, bay leaves, and thyme

A small handful of whole peppercorns

4 whole leeks, sliced into halves if small, into quarters if large

1 turnip per person, peeled and chopped into halves or quarters

1 head cabbage, cored and cut into wedges

1 beef marrowbone per person (about 1½ inches each)

Cornichons, served as a side, with mustard, for the table

Serves 6

- Fill a large saucepan with cold water and add salt.

- Place the meat in the saucepan, and then add a carrot and the
  onion, garlic, celery, bouquet garni, pepper, and some of the green
  bits of the leeks to make a stock.

- Cover and bring to a simmer and cook on medium heat for around
  3 hours.

- While it's simmering, check frequently and use a spoon to skim off
  any impurities and grease.

- Leave it to cool and place in the fridge overnight.

- The next day, scrape off the layer of grease that has formed on the
  surface. Place the saucepan back on the stove on low heat and put
  a steamer on top of the saucepan.

- Put the remaining carrots and the turnips in the steamer and cook
  for about 15 minutes. Then add the cabbage and the remaining
  leeks and continue to cook for another 10 to 15 minutes. But don't
  overcook—the vegetables should be firm.

- Dab the ends of the beef marrowbones in salt, and wrap each piece in aluminum foil.

- Fill a saucepan with water, set on high heat, and add salt and pepper. When the water is boiling, add the bone marrow pieces and bring down to a simmer for 10 minutes.

- After removing the garlic and the bouquet garni, serve the meat and marrowbones in one dish and the vegetables in another, with the bouillon on the side.

- Don't forget to bring out the mustard and cornichons for the table.

After talking about sex, the topic of conversation that goes best with dessert is adultery. It's a universal subject; everyone will have an opinion or an experience to share and you can be sure that none of your guests will be bored.

— I'd much rather my boyfriend have a one-night stand than a platonic romantic attachment.

— I agree. You don't leave someone because you've cheated on them; you leave because you're not in love with them anymore. Technically, fantasizing is cheating.

— But I spend my life fantasizing. When I'm making love I think of my boxing coach, my PhD student, my neighbor . . . It's just my imagination, it has nothing to do with reality.

— But that's not what I'm talking about! I mean imagine there was one guy in particular who you thought about every time you're in bed with your boyfriend . . . Don't you see it's completely different?

There are as many recipes for chocolate cake as there are Parisiennes in Paris. However you prefer it—more or less sweet, gooey, or rich—it doesn't matter. There's nothing better than a good chocolate fondant to accompany a little talk on infidelity.

CHOCOLATE FONDANT

INGREDIENTS
1 stick and 1 tablespoon butter
7½ ounces very dark bittersweet chocolate
4 eggs
½ cup sugar
½ cup flour

Serves 6
Prep time: 15 minutes
Cooking time: 30 minutes plus 10 minutes for cooling

· Preheat the oven to 350°F.

· Melt the butter and the chocolate in a bain-marie (place the butter and chocolate in a bowl, then place the bowl in a saucepan of boiling water to melt them together. If using the microwave, use a larger bowl filled with water).

· In a separate bowl, use an electric mixer to beat the eggs with the sugar and then add the flour.

· Fold the chocolate/butter mixture into the egg mixture.

· Pour the mixture into a round medium-sized baking pan and bake for 30 minutes at 350°F, then leave to cool for 10 minutes before serving. To check, slide a knife in and if it comes out clean, your cake is ready.

Parisian dinner parties often end later than a night out clubbing. Heated debates, outrageous statements, dramatic turns of event . . . anything goes to keep boredom at bay. But the best part of the evening is yet to come. When the guests leave, it's not time to go to sleep straightaway but to dissect the evening. They don't wait until they're in bed, or call one another the next day on their lunch breaks—the debriefing begins as soon as the guests walk out the door.

— Françoise and Jean-Paul seem to be doing much better.

— I know. Sleeping with his best friend has really put the fire back into their relationship.

— You mean he's cheating on her with another man?

— Sweetheart, I'd be even more surprised if it were the other way around.

— Françoise is such a great hostess . . .

— Is that a good enough reason not to say anything about the Saint-Émilion being corked?

— It wasn't the wine—everyone knows you shouldn't serve a *pot-au-feu* with a Bordeaux—it ruins the taste. But you're right, the wine was corked.

— Marie wasn't drinking, do you think she's pregnant?

— Uh uh. At her age?

— She didn't look great.

— My dear, haven't you heard of the affliction that will catch up with us all one day? It's called age.

— That Georges . . . he's so mysterious. He's a writer, isn't he?

— Honey, don't be fooled: he stays silent so as to give himself airs. As Sacha Guitry used to say, "You can pretend to be serious, but you cannot pretend to be witty."

— Don't be so mean; he's Catherine's deaf brother!

— NO WAY! I always thought she'd invented him to stop us teasing her about having an only-child syndrome.

Good night, my friends, and sweet dreams. And don't forget to drink a gallon of water before going to sleep—it's the best way to avoid a hangover.

COOL
OR COLD?

Never wear your glasses, especially if you're nearsighted. That way, you won't have to acknowledge people you know. You'll have that aloof look, the one that seduces men (but annoys women because they see right through you).

When invited to parties, be the last to arrive. Sip your champagne, but never get too drunk.

Always look as if you are gazing at the sunset. Even during rush hour in the Métro. Even when picking up frozen pizza from the supermarket.

When on the phone, no need for small talk. "Hi, how are you." Get to the point. Hang up as soon as you have your answer. End all of your calls with "See you later," even with people you won't see for another year.

Talk softly so that people have to lean in to hear you. Look preoccupied. Speak in quotes.

Give yourself over but don't give yourself away.

Of course you run the risk of ending up alone. And all because you were oblivious to the man who could have held you in his arms, and ignored the awkward-looking girl who could have been a lifelong friend.

If that's the case, you can always book a one-way ticket to Paris.

Where Does This
Pout Come From?

To the delight of visitors and the dismay of the locals, Paris is an open-air museum. Each street is steeped in history; each cobblestone carries the weight of tradition. The ghosts of our Parisian ancestors, their wandering souls, look down from the gargoyles above, taunting us with their cry: "Will you be up to it?"

The *précieuses* belong to these lingering ancestors. During the reigns of Louis XIII and Louis XIV, some women of the court created a feminist movement to fight against the prevailing misogyny of the era. These women sought tenderness and restraint. They wanted to hear sweet nothings whispered in their ears—to be charmed and won over with wit and grace, before being whisked off to bed.

The writer Madeleine de Scudéry was the leader of this movement. She drew a map of an imaginary country called Tenderness. In order to reach the city of Love, one had to pass through several small villages, each one a new step toward winning the heart of one's beloved.

From these first feminists, the Parisiennes have kept the characteristically cold, slightly aloof pout. It is part of our heritage, just like a delicately placed beauty spot or an antique chest of drawers, passed down from one generation to the next.

Even today, the Map of Tenderness lives on subconsciously in the heart of a Parisienne. She can shift from hot to cold, from indifference to friendship, exploring the twists and turns that are essential to any journey in human relationships. Things develop over time, but you need quiet strength to nurture strong ties. Although the Parisienne does not extend her affection lightly, once offered, it lasts till death do us part, "cross my heart and hope to die."

Parisian Snobbisms

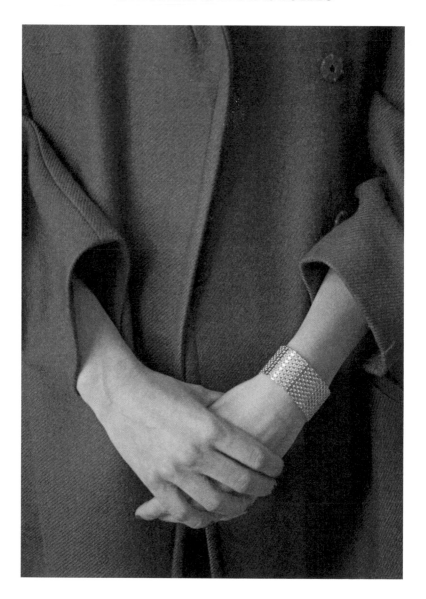

* On New Year's Eve, enjoy a plate of oysters at home and go to bed before midnight. (The pre–New Year's Eve party you hosted last night was already the "best of the year.")

* Never say *"Bon Appétit!"* when you sit down for a meal. (And never pass the salt directly—place it on the table first for the other person to pick up.)

* Leave a party when it's in full swing. (Even your own.)

* Wear navy blue with black. (And red with pink, à la Yves Saint Laurent.)

* When meeting someone for the first time, never say "What a pleasure," but rather "What a pleasure to meet you." (You never know what the future might hold.)

* Say "The Search" (when referring to Proust's *In Search of Lost Time*).

* Don't use abbreviations when texting. (And emoticons should be only for your girlfriends.)

* Don't follow trends. (Trends follow you.)

* Never lose control. (But make sure you have a steamy past.)

* Be friends with people of different generations. (Both young and old, but especially the old.)

* Embrace your inner snob. (Because let's face it, that's who you are.)

AN OFF DAY AT WORK

She's lying in bed. Her alarm went off a while ago, but she's not moving. There is no good reason for her to be wasting this precious time, other than a pressing sense that she need not hurry. People will no doubt be waiting for her at work. She muses over this while she takes a shower, and only then does it occur to her what a late night she had. But as soon as she is outside and on the street, she's caught up in the rhythm of the crowd. She feels a surge of guilt that makes her run for the bus. During the whole ride, she racks her brain for possible alibis, dismissing the ones she already used the past few weeks. As the minutes pass, a palpable anxiety forms in her stomach. So much so that as she reaches her office door, flushed and out of breath, she has real tears in her eyes. And nobody dreams of asking what might have happened at home to provoke such a tired look so early in the morning. This creates a vicious cycle, for the compassionate looks she inspires make her feel that her soul is truly aching.

Sitting at her desk, she's working but not really there. Letting her fingers dance over the keyboard, she remembers the face of the man she did not go home with last night, the guy who didn't even kiss her in the end. She concludes that you can indeed be orphaned by a fantasy and feel abandoned by a perfect stranger. When her colleague comes over with a work-related question, she gives the wrong answer but lands on her feet somehow, ducking the issue. And when the woman across from her points this out, she loses it, which startles everyone, not least herself. For the rest of the day nobody is inclined to approach her. Sobered by her own temper, she buckles down and gets everything done with the drive of a woman determined to prove her worth to the world. She focuses on a difficult negotiation and refuses, as a matter of pride, to back down. When she walks out, chin high, she has the fierce allure of someone who's emerging from battle . . . She might even grab a drink on her way home. After all, she deserves it.

HARD TO ADMIT

A Parisienne never hires a babysitter who is too pretty, always finding the less attractive one to be far more competent.

She often murmurs, with feigned discomfort, that she's a bit worried that her daughter is "rather precocious." It's her way of saying that her child is a genius—or that she takes after her mother.

She often pretends her child is sick in order to get out of dinner parties that will bore her to death. Then she feels guilty, and worries that some god will actually make her baby ill, to punish her for her lies.

She doesn't balk at changing diapers but she never mentions the nasty details of stomach bugs or other ailments in public. Even at the pediatrician's she is reluctant to pronounce those words out loud.

She doesn't automatically breast-feed her children—only if she wants to. And anyone who tells her what she should or shouldn't do with her breasts had better beware. Particularly if he's a man . . .

She occasionally lets her children sleep in her bed, especially because all the parenting books ever written forbid it and because she likes to stand out from the crowd . . .

She buys time with candy, so that she can finish her phone conversation with her best friend.

She quite likes some of her children's friends, but others she thinks are real idiots. And she makes no particular effort to hide her opinion—being hypocritical would just be setting a bad example.

She can spend hours playing make-believe with her little ones. She'd be quite happy to live in one of their imaginary worlds forever, if only she didn't have to return to the adult life to earn a living.

NOT YOUR MOST
GLORIOUS MOMENTS

* It's the text message you send the very girl you are writing nasty stuff about. Simply because you were thinking of her so much that you accidentally selected her name.

* Worse: It's hearing yourself try to apologize to this girl, who doesn't believe for a second that you're sorry and is listening only for the pleasure of making you squirm.

* It's the charming guy you run into at a party for the second time, who comes up to you smiling, and says "Hi, Anne." Your name is Audrey.

* It's the pantyhose that rip just as you sit down for a job interview. You focus so much on the hole in your stockings that it becomes a hole in your memory, which turns into a hole in your bank account when you don't get the job.

* It's the pork roast you prepared for tonight's dinner party, forgetting that your friends are practicing Muslims.

* It's the alarm on your phone that goes off in the middle of your 11:00 a.m. meeting reminding you to take your birth control. Best-case scenario, the guy sitting across from you thinks this is when you normally wake up.

* It's the morning after, when you open your eyes next to someone and remember that you never did take that birth control, because you were in said 11:00 a.m. meeting.

* It's when your father sends you that raunchy message meant for his mistress. And you promptly get over your Oedipus complex.

* It's champagne. Vodka. Champagne. Vodka. Champagne. Until it's time to drink coffee.

* It's the embarrassing photo you have no recollection of taking that somehow made it to the office before you. Thanks, Twitter.

* It's realizing you're the one who posted it. *Merde.*

* It's the 456 unread messages in your work in-box.

* It's the message from a headhunter you received a year ago but never saw among all those e-mails.

* It's your banker being the first person to call you on your birthday.

* It's the taxman being the second, as if they were in cahoots.

* It's the pimple on your behind on date night.

  Not your most glorious moments, but important because they prevent you from ever taking yourself too seriously.

HOW TO DESTABILIZE A MAN

She:

cancels a date at the last minute and apologizes, but won't give him a reason.

describes her evening in five words or fewer ("It was really fun"), and then goes straight to bed.

talks politics with her mouth and sex with her eyes.

is alarmingly honest and answers "terribly" when asked how she's doing.

actually forgets to wear a bra in summertime.

makes an office meeting more exciting by discreetly laying her hand on his thigh.

settles her scores with sex, instead of talking it through.

grabs hold of a stranger's arm to walk down the stairs in heels.

manages to pay the bill before he even asks for it.

randomly exclaims, "This is the most wonderful day of my life!"

THE 6:00 P.M. DEBATE
THE GYM

This is a story that begins with an inner debate. As the workday draws to a close, the dilemma sets in. *Does she really have to go to the gym?* It just so happens that as the result of a previous internal debate brought on by an afternoon spent with her mother, she signed up for a gym membership. Her mother had been so beautiful (family photos attest to her former long-limbed elegance). And yet, a mere decade of inactivity was all it took to ruin this gift that Mother Nature had so graciously bestowed upon her. As she watched her mother making coffee that afternoon with heavy hips and a sagging backside that had succumbed to Newton's law, it became clear to her that the god who had invented menopause was obviously a misogynist. And so she made a serious decision that fateful day: it was time she join a gym and defy her genetic baggage and the laws of gravity.

Uneasy and hesitant, she had entered a gym gloriously underprepared, in a pair of old Converses and sweatpants that she never wears. She signed up, adding her name forever to the official registry of sporty girls. Once inside the fortress she felt even less sure of herself, but vowed not to let it show. She refused to ask for help with the treadmill settings, and, consequently, ended up running at an awkward speed, clumsily stretching one leg out in front of the other, not unlike a duck, too proud to stop before the allocated fifteen minutes were up. Her panting betrayed her thirty years of careless living: cigarettes, alcohol, and a chronic lack of sleep. Despite the cramps, she stuck it out like a warrior. After twenty-three minutes, she leaves the gym proud and vowing to return soon.

That was a month ago. The dilemma has continued to haunt her every day since. **She thinks of her mother's backside and the cost of the gym membership, but that's not enough.** Come six o'clock, a wave of exhaustion overwhelms her and she feels the dangerous draw of the sidewalk café. And, just then, her friends call her up, as if to test her willpower. She knows she doesn't have much resolve, and deep down, she doesn't really give a damn. She makes a mental note to go to the gym the next day. She curses her mother for losing her figure, causing her daughter anxiety attacks (though thankfully these are easily dispelled). At 7:00 p.m., she is holding a glass of red wine in her hand, and the idea of working out is long gone.

SCENES FROM PARISIAN LIFE: TAKE 2

_BUT
YOU TOLD HIM
NEVER
TO CALL YOU
AGAIN!

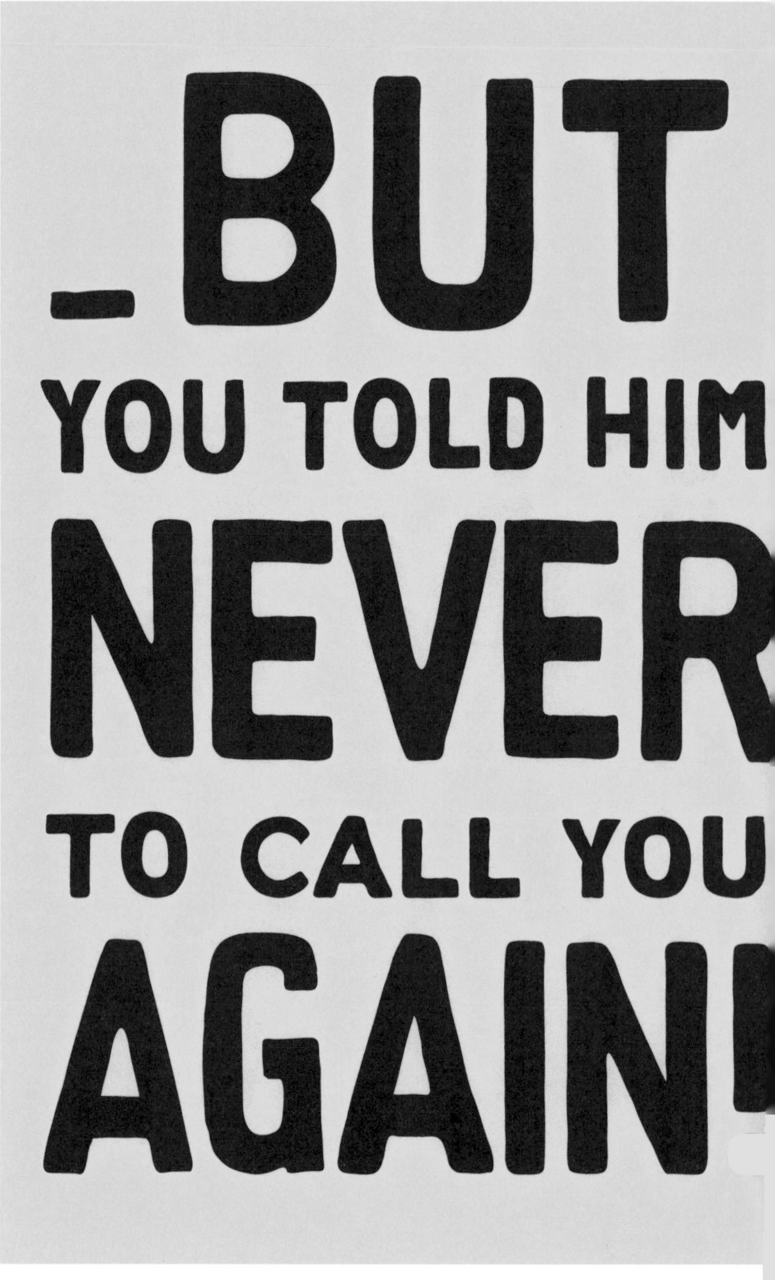

...I JUST CAN'T BELIEVE HE *ACTUALLY* LISTENED.

3

CULTIVATE YOUR ALLURE

24-Hour
Look

THE
ESSENTIALS

Jeans, anytime, anywhere, and any way. Take a Parisienne's jeans out of her closet and she feels stark naked.

Men's shoes. Simply because everyone says that these chic, flat shoes aren't meant for women but you're a contrarian by nature. In fact, that's the very essence of your style.

The bag. It's not an accessory, it's your home. It's an indispensable shambles, where you're just as likely to find a shriveled up four-leaf clover as an old electricity bill. If it's beautiful on the outside, that's just to keep up appearances. And so that no one ever wonders what's inside.

The little black blazer. It smartens up a scruffy pair of jeans (the ones you wear all the time) and you wear it on days when you don't want to make it look too obvious that you don't feel like making an effort.

Ballet flats. Your equivalent of slippers. You don't choose between comfort and elegance; for you, it's all or nothing. Nobody ever saw Audrey Hepburn wearing carpet slippers.

A small silk scarf. It has more than one function. First, it adds a touch of color to a dark outfit without running the risk of a fashion faux pas. Then, when it rains, you wear it over your head like Romy Schneider. And, on occasion, you can even use it to wipe your child's nose when you've run out of tissues.

The white shirt. It's iconic and timeless.

A long trench, of course, for warmer weather. You know it doesn't keep you as warm as a down jacket. But when you put on a down jacket, you feel like you're voluntarily adding extra love handles.

A thick scarf. Precisely because you don't own a parka. And despite pretending otherwise, sometimes you get cold.

The oversized sweater that slips off your shoulder. You wear it the day after a party, as if you're snuggled up in a quilt. It's as soft as a teddy bear, as calming as a Xanax, as wide as a screen, perfect for days when you can feel your hips too much.

Basic oversized sunglasses. Every day, even when it's raining, because you always have a reason to wear them: too bright out, a hangover, tears running down your face, a desire to be mysterious . . .

An oversized shirt. You always undo one extra button so it doesn't look too serious. In general, you borrow your boyfriend's. You'll never return it and you may even one day wear it in somebody else's arms. Love can fade, but some fashion lasts forever.

The very simple, but very expensive T-shirt. This contradiction guides your life like *Liberty Leading the People;* you're perfectly happy to give in to the most common trends, as long as you can add a mark of luxury. As a result you spend hours searching for the perfect T-shirt, whose finely woven and slightly transparent thread make it feel like cashmere.

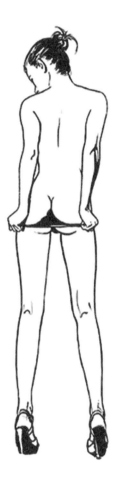

marel.

LESS IS MORE

Zsa Zsa Gabor used to say: "The only place men want depth in their women is in their décolletage."

She may have been right, but too much cleavage leaves too little to the imagination. It's like serving dessert before anyone has even touched their appetizer. It tries too hard, shows its hand too quickly, and betrays a certain lack of self-confidence. Like a girl who talks so incessantly there's nothing left to ask.

The Parisienne never gives too much away. When it comes to revealing herself, she follows one golden rule: less is definitely more.

A skirt that rides ever so slightly up her thigh when she sits down in a café; a wide-necked tee that slips down her shoulder as she waves for the waiter; the surreptitious hint of her breasts when she leans down to pick up her bag.

Just an inch, a small dose.

This small dose fires up the imagination of the beholder. It makes him desperate to find out what comes next, to hear the woman's story, to break through her silences, to tear off her shirt . . . This woman deals out her mystery with restraint, and only gives access to the enigma of her body in gradual increments. And many are those who are desperate to throw themselves at her feet, for a chance to slip off her heels. One inch. No more.

On a Parisienne's Bookshelf

THERE ARE MANY BOOKS ON A PARISIENNE'S BOOKSHELF:

* The books you so often claim you've read that you actually believe you have.

* The books you read in school from which you remember only the main character's name.

* The crime novels that your boyfriend devours, which you'll never admit to owning.

* The art books your parents give you each Christmas so you can get some "culture."

* The art books that you bought yourself and which you really love.

* The books that you've been promising yourself you'll read next summer . . . for the past ten years.

* The books you bought only because you liked the title.

* The books that you think make you cool.

* The books you read over and over again, and that evolve along with your life.

* The books that remind you of someone you loved.

* The books you keep for your children, just in case you ever have any.

* The books whose first ten pages you've read so many times you know them by heart.

* The books you own simply because you must and, taken together, form intangible proof that you are well read.

AND THEN THERE ARE THE BOOKS YOU HAVE READ, LOVED, AND WHICH ARE A PART OF YOUR IDENTITY:

The Stranger, Albert Camus

The Elementary Particles, Michel Houellebecq

Belle du Seigneur, Albert Cohen

Bonjour Tristesse, Françoise Sagan

Madame Bovary, Gustave Flaubert

Foam of the Daze, Boris Vian

Lolita, Vladimir Nabokov

The Flowers of Evil, Charles Baudelaire

Journey to the End of the Night, Louis-Ferdinand Céline

Swann's Way, Marcel Proust

Louis Aragon Aurélien
Baudelaire Les Fleurs du Mal
Marc Dugain Une exécution ordinaire
Kundera La plaisanterie
Albert Cohen Solal
Patrick Modiano Dora Bruder
Joseph Kessel Contes
Marcel Proust Le Temps retrouvé
Le Clézio Désert
Guy Debord La Société du Spectacle
Jacques Prévert Paroles
Philip Roth Professeur de désir
Raymond Queneau Le chiendent
Camus L'étranger
François Furet Penser la Révolution française
Alexandre Dumas La reine Margot
Sartre Les mains sales
Kundera L'insoutenable légèreté de l'être
Sartre L'imaginaire
Romain Gary La vie devant soi
Kundera L'art du roman
Nathalie Sarraute Martereau
William Faulkner Lumière d'août
Sartre La nausée
Raymond Chandler La dame du lac
Camus La chute
Marguerite Duras La douleur
Daniel Pennac Monsieur Malaussène
Marcel Proust Un amour de Swann
Borges Fictions
BAUDELAIRE LES FLEURS DU MAL
PLATON LA RÉPUBLIQUE
LACLOS LES LIAISONS DANGEREUSES
ÉRASME ÉLOGE DE LA FOLIE

THE MINISKIRT

W hether you're pairing it with a white tee or a patterned blouse, you must never wear a miniskirt with any hint of décolletage or vulgarity. Keep your heels low and your makeup invisible. To be worthy of the name, a miniskirt must be perfectly cut. Whether it is denim, cotton, or leather, it should be straight and classically simple.

In France, the miniskirt is not about wanting to seduce. Instead it's a symbol of freedom. The miniskirt was born in Paris, long before London's swinging sixties (at least that's what the Parisiennes like to believe). The first was commissioned from fashion designer Jean Patou in the early 1920s, when French tennis champion Suzanne Lenglen asked him to design a skirt for her to wear in the Olympics. It set a new standard, of strong women competing in a man's world, without relinquishing their femininity.

Ever since, the miniskirt has held a pivotal position in the back-and-forth between *hide and show* . . . It captures that perfect moment between dressed and undressed—neither naked, nor concealed, that sweet spot between the two.

"Women's legs are like compass points, circling the globe and providing its balance and harmony."

—from François Truffaut's *The Man Who Loved Women* (*L'Homme qui aimait les femmes*, 1977)

SAVE YOUR SKIN

What *wouldn't* you do for your skin? Of all the precious fabrics you love, your skin is without a doubt the one that fascinates you most of all. The one that you care for and cherish. You can read its every wrinkle like lines on parchment. The relationship that binds you to your skin is the fruit of a lifelong education.

Beauty in France is epidermal—nobody cares that much about makeup, it's what's underneath that matters. Early on, your mother gave you a magnifying mirror: a window on aging and the passage of time. She didn't repeatedly warn you not to smoke, not to drink too much, she simply invited you to view their side effects in your reflection. Your skin retains the memory of every party you ever went to, under your eyes and at the corners of your lips. That is how she taught you to be wary of your penchant for excess.

In Paris, the rules are clear: you anticipate, you prepare for the future, but you *never* totally correct. Play with what nature gave you. Make the most of it. This is what your mother passed on to you. Along with her science of creams that verge on witchcraft. You've never counted the number of jars in your bathroom but you know there is one for every inch of your face and then some: from your neck and your breasts all the way to the soles of your feet.

Your first few hangovers aside—now you never go to bed without taking off your makeup, so you fall asleep not smelling like the party. Yes, you climb into bed more tired from this care. But that's the price we pay to save our skin.

When You Can Have Anything

She doesn't have a ring on each finger, or a big diamond on each ring.

She doesn't wear a gold watch that costs as much as a fancy car.

In fact, she doesn't own a fancy car.

She doesn't carry an enormous designer bag.

But she might have a newspaper under her arm.

She might mention Sartre or Foucault in a conversation.

It's her personality that sparkles and nothing else: the signs of intellectual wealth.

Women in Black

HEADS.

If her wardrobe is made up only of black, it's not because she's in mourning. Quite the contrary. Black is the color of celebration, the color of nights that never end, of women who pull the blinds to shut out the dawn. A long, dark silhouette, slender and elegant, walking through a crowd of long, dark silhouettes, slender and elegant. That is the definition of a party here. And it seems that a tacit agreement on this code is shared by all those on the streets past midnight. Even white can appear like a stain on this darkened tableau. But don't think this image is monotonous: Paris has found a name for this particular style. Words that come from the mouth of the man who, alone, seems to have invented black, Yves Saint Laurent. He used to say, "There's not one black, but many blacks." He managed to convince people that this achromatic style is a subtle art. If God made light, it seems that Saint Laurent turned it off just as successfully.

TAILS.

In truth, you must scratch below the surface to find the true meaning of this implacable darkness. Behind her posturing, the Parisienne hides a fear, a frenzied panic: that she is not chic. That she'll commit a faux pas, because black is practical and convenient. It's a safe bet—even for a woman with no eye for fashion. Black is comfortable and all-purpose. It sharpens contours and compensates for poor taste. It is your nighttime insurance, the promise of losing yourself among the fashionable masses. When you think about it, this trend epitomizes her herd instinct, the (black) sheep side of her. But don't count on her to admit that she's wearing a uniform. And be aware that you'll gain nothing by pointing out this kind of truth to her. If you do, you'll only blacken her mood. She'll stare you up and down, turn on her heels, and disappear into the shadows forever.

OFF
THE
RADAR

You are drinking your coffee alone at a sidewalk café.

You are watching people around you, families, children playing, a young woman engrossed in a book, a lost tourist trying to find his way, a man in a hurry, running to catch his bus, the leaves of the cherry tree above your head.

You have no real reason to be there: you're not meeting anyone, and no one is waiting for you elsewhere. You will stay as long as you like, and leave only when you're ready. On a whim you can decide what to do and how to do it: there is something a bit dangerous and yet delicious about freedom.

You are anonymous in your own city; no one knows your age, who you are, or what you do for a living. In this moment, you can regain control of your life. Feel the beating of your heart, take a deep breath, and listen to yourself. Do nothing. Absolutely nothing. Savor these stolen moments. They help you regroup, and belong to no one else. You alone are responsible for what happens to you.

Nowadays more than ever your life is organized like clockwork, everything's planned, you go from A to B, yet at this instant your phone is turned off, no one knows what you're doing or where you are. It's exciting to break your own habits; you're cheating on yourself, expanding the scope of your possibilities.

You could just disappear. Jump into a cab and take a plane to Caracas or Ulan Bator, or simply spend all day at the movies. Or you could strike up a conversation with the woman sitting next to you in the café, even though you'd normally be too shy, and you could ask her about her book, say, "Oh, no, I've never read Turgenev," and then talk about how the neighborhood has changed. Resume your wander, stop in a park; answer when a stranger chats you up. Why not? You'll never see him again. He won't know your name, where you come from, your brothers' or your sisters' names, how much you hate your ears, why you once cheated on an important math exam, or why you prefer making love in the morning. Just share this moment, suspended in time, before slowly heading home.

You turn your phone back on, read your messages, and send word to reassure the people in your life who were worried when you became momentarily silent.

Ennui is your secret garden.

And solitude can be a luxury.

NAVY BLUE

In the eighties, this familiar tune could be heard over and over again on the radio, "I reached rock bottom of the pool, in my little navy sweater, with its rips at the elbows that I chose never to re-sew."

We grew up on this refrain; we all imagined a stunningly beautiful girl in distress, with a V-neck sweater that matched the color of her eyes. We've all wanted to steal that sweater from her, despite its holes, since it's impossible to borrow her eyes. If we exaggerate a little, we could say that Isabelle Adjani invented navy blue. Or rather, that Serge Gainsbourg, who wrote this cult song, invented it for her. Gainsbourg was a mischievous lover. A painter at heart, he went so far as to corrupt a color for a woman, a color that until then in France was largely associated with firefighters' uniforms. And, as is often the case, the Parisienne agrees with Serge. This particular blue is the one she's adopted: it's the color of her jeans, of the thick scarf she ties around her neck in winter, of the trench that falls just below her knee, or the stripes of her favorite sailor top. This blue is the color of the depth of night, the tint that is closest to black, the black that we cherish so much. To the point of breaking one of fashion's most absolute commandments: Thou shalt not pair black with blue. A discreet rebellion, feeble at best. But the Parisienne doesn't care, she prefers mystery to demonstration. At least, that's how she consoles herself for this certain lack of imagination. And not unlike Adjani, she's content with adding an accessory to her overly sober style: "wearing smoky shades to show everything I want to hide."

The Parisienne
as Seen by an
American Novelist

"They zigzagged across the city, in evening's flattering light. Parisians looked good already; now they looked even better. The restaurant Claire took them to, in the Latin Quarter's narrow streets, was small and hectic, the walls covered in Moroccan tiles. Mitchell sat facing the window, watching the people streaming past outside. At one point, a girl who looked to be in her early twenties, with a Joan of Arc haircut, passed right in front of the glass. When Mitchell looked at her, the girl did an amazing thing: she looked back. She met his gaze with frank sexual meaning. Not that she *wanted* to have sex with him, necessarily. Only that she was happy to acknowledge, on this late-summer evening, that he was a man and she a woman, and if he found her attractive, that was all right with her."

—from *The Marriage Plot* by Jeffrey Eugenides

The Simones

All Parisiennes have a Simone in their past. The city is divided into three distinct categories: the Simone Veils, the Simone de Beauvoirs, and the Simone Signorets. The three spend time together, talk, sometimes even like one another. But deep down each believes that they are from a different family, and prefer those who share a secret bond. However, they are first cousins all the same and this sense of clan is more snobbery than true rivalry. Let us explain.

THE SIMONE VEILS

This woman is first and foremost a survivor. Simone Veil was in the concentration camps of Drancy, Auschwitz-Birkenau, and Bergen-Belsen, and made it out alive. But her name became part of history the day abortion was decriminalized in France. Veil, then minister of health, fought to give women the right to choose. This fight earned her serious threats from the far right but, naturally, that didn't stop her.

Simone Veil is the archetype of the intelligent woman who fights for her peers. A feminist, hotheaded, unwavering, she is a model for all politically aware women who yearn for a better world. She has rallied a myriad of educated young women to spend their weekends swelling the ranks of excited demonstrations (France's national sport). For some, however, this engagement has mostly become a way of defining themselves, giving them a sense of style, akin to a teenager going goth.

MANTRA: *"My demand as a woman is that my difference be taken into account and that I not be forced to adapt to the male model."*

THE SIMONE DE BEAUVOIRS

She embodies this very French way of loving, of being a "wife of" without disappearing behind a spouse's name. Simone de Beauvoir may well have shared Jean-Paul Sartre's life, but she left her own unforgettable mark, a writer renowned and much loved in her country. She too was a feminist, but she grew up with a father who would say—meaning it as a compliment—"You have the brain of a man, my girl." Although she was a diehard Communist, she was a secret romantic who was always wary of yielding to her emotions. The book she wrote about her partner's final years, *La Cérémonie des Adieux* (published in English as *Adieux: A Farewell to Sartre*), shocked readers with the bluntness of its details. De Beauvoir is the ideal for seductive warriors who like to please without giving the impression they care too much for that kind of thing.

> MANTRA: *"She did not try to make others happy; she selfishly delighted in the pleasure of giving pleasure."*

THE SIMONE SIGNORETS

She is the sacrificial heroine, who, like the Little Mermaid, would be willing to give up everything, from her legs to her voice, for the man she loved. For Simone Signoret, that man was Yves Montand, one of the greatest French actors of all time. Together, they exuded movie glamour. She was an actress and writer, with a searching look and scarlet lips. He was a playboy of Italian descent with a disarming smile. Though Signoret won the Oscar for Best Actress for her role in *Room at the Top* in 1960, that same year her husband was in *Let's Make Love* and everyone knew, herself included, that he was having an affair with Marilyn Monroe. However, Signoret didn't leave him. She waited, acting as though nothing was wrong, suffering in silence. She broke this silence only much later. After Yves came back to her, after Marilyn's death. She would say about Marilyn, "My one regret was never telling her that I didn't bear her a grudge." All

the hopeless romantics of the nation have at one point or another coveted her particular kind of courage, this martyr for love, whose tale has a happy ending: she and Yves rest side by side in the Père Lachaise Cemetery.

MANTRA: *"The secret to happiness in love is not being blind, but knowing when to close your eyes."*

In the
Countryside

As she climbs out of the car, she feels a slight sense of unease come over her. The Parisienne lives by only one sound: that of her heels clicking on the pavement, setting a steady tempo for her life. She knows the rhythm well, it's the metronome of her days. However, no sooner does she set foot in the countryside than the sole of her shoe sinks into damp grass and she realizes she is on foreign soil.

Truth be told, she likes green meadows only in paintings, like those old canvases hanging in her parents' living room—no need for more. With each step, she feels the unraveling of the electric wires that connect to her world. She loses reception: Internet, telephone. She's hot, she's cold, she's at the mercy of the seasons, and dreads the smell of her own perspiration. She has now truly left her comfort zone. For her, the country is nothing more than the sum of its missing parts. Finally, she likes things natural, but not nature itself. If her cheeks are rosy, it's only because she's wearing blush. If she smells of flowers, it's because she's wearing tuberose-scented perfume. Yes, she'll admit that her charm is somewhat artificial. *Et alors?*

With an already less assured step, she heads toward a building she recognizes as a farmhouse. Or maybe not. To be honest, she is no longer sure of anything. Slowly she becomes more aware of her surroundings. She can hear a swarm of wasps buzzing above her head. The terrifying soundtrack of this hostile wildlife reminds her of her own fragility. A fly flits across her shirt. As she takes off her shoes, she walks on a patch of stinging nettles.

The Parisienne, who cherishes the civilized world above all, can't help but be appalled by Mother Nature's intrusive ways. *Bien sûr,* she is overreacting, but this is the only weapon she has left to defend her persona.

She sits down on a bench in front of the farmhouse and closes her eyes, letting the wind caress her face. When she stops complaining to herself for a moment, she feels an exquisite light-headedness rush over her. She appreciates the simplicity of these minutes alone. She even delights in the splendor of a hundred-year-old tree that could rival the grandeur of certain cathedrals. But she'd never admit to this. Defending the countryside would mean renouncing the city, changing religions, running the risk of being excommunicated, and becoming forever after the poor little Parisienne who got lost in a field of wheat.

THE BEST VERSION
OF YOURSELF

Once you reach a certain stage in life, "you have the face that you deserve." Coco Chanel wasn't one to mince her words and her cruelty was legendary. Nevertheless, in the collective Parisian psyche, a few things ring true.

In the street, at a café, on the bus, a person's face can tell a story, like a crystal ball that reveals the past. Happy or long-lost loves, births, hopes, and victories, successes interwoven with twists of fate.

Experiences, and the ways in which we change, become our visual identity. Everything is laid out for the world to see. We are either born lucky, with a face that suits us. Or not.

But life often rights wrongs. The pretty girls who were queen bees in high school, who had everything handed to them on a platter, and rested on their laurels, are eclipsed by the ones they never see coming: the ones who turn their difference into an asset, a trademark. And like any good vintage, they get better with age.

And these women have learned the immutable facts: swimming against the current gets you nowhere, you must go with the flow.

Better to look your age than look no age at all. By now we've learned that relying on excessive plastic surgery ages you more than real life. Sure, some women sometimes master the art of Botox, but most of the time, let's be honest: instead of a face free of wrinkles, what you really see is the face of fear.

Parisian women never try to appear to be something other than what they are. In truth, more than wanting to look young—which is but a fleeting illusion—they want above all to become the best possible version of themselves, outside and in, at any age.

In their mind, a single rule outweighs all others: enjoy the face you have today. It's the one you'll wish you have ten years from now.

Take the time to talk to the elderly lady next door, to read a book, to walk to work instead of riding the subway when it's a beautiful day. Take the time to escape for a weekend with friends.

Take the time to listen and to get to know yourself. Take the time to change, to grow, to rest. Take the time to say yes, take the time to say no. Take the time to be quiet. Take the time to look after your body, to eat well. Take the time to ask yourself who you are and what you want.

Call your grandmother on her birthday and rinse your hair with cold water just like she taught you, listen to your children, breathe deeply, take the time to make fresh-squeezed orange juice for breakfast, to go to a museum, to go for a stroll in the woods and to listen to the sounds of tiny creatures in the grass. In summer, take the time to compile a scrapbook of pressed flowers with a child, to read him a story.

Take the time to take time because nobody else will do it for you.

And don't forget to daydream in the bath, just like when you were little.

TAKE
YOUR
TIME

Trinkets and Treasures

The Parisienne wears very little jewelry.

The Inseparable: a fine chain, a simple ring, a family heirloom. It is as discreet as possible, and should subtly suit you. It's your trademark.

The Statement Piece: a chunky gold bracelet or a gemstone necklace, these statement pieces are for brightening up a casual daytime outfit or for wearing on the beach with a tan.

The Theory of Contrasts: the smarter the outfit, the less jewelry you need.

"The Jewels," by Baudelaire: "My well-beloved was stripped. Knowing my whim, / She wore her tinkling gems, but naught besides." Take a leaf out of his book and keep your jewelry on in bed. Whether you're going to sleep or making love. It will give you sweet dreams.

The Authentic Fake: don't shy away from costume jewelry. Wear your bargains with pride. The Parisienne wears the Authentic Fake on a night out because she doesn't care if it's stolen on the Métro. But she wouldn't dream of wearing anything "fake authentic." Knockoff luxury pieces are heresy.

Your Watch: it is also considered a piece of jewelry. That doesn't mean it has to cost a fortune, only that it should be pretty, classic, or quirky. Your watch completes an outfit, either by perking it up or by adding contrast.

The Backstory: you don't need to own a lot of jewelry, but each piece—whether a memento from your family or your travels—should tell a story. Their value lies not in their price but in their sentiment.

– Are you WORKING OUT?

Nope. I don't have TIME

SO what are you doing about IT?

I'm going to buy myself a LONG COAT.

4

DARE TO LOVE

THE IDEAL MAN

He's not muscular. (You'd rather think of him reading a book than lifting weights.)

He's unshaven. (Just enough so that you never fully see the man behind the stubble.)

He's clean. (But makes sure it's not too obvious.)

He's funny. (Until he disappears.)

He's got something special. (And it's not a car.)

He's got class. (But it's unintentional.)

He's a bad boy. (But you always forgive him.)

He may not be perfect, but at least he really exists.

AN OPTIMISTIC
VIEW ON LOVE

In general, love stories end badly.

You've known this for as long as you can remember—but that's not all. You've also repeatedly been told that you're going to fall in love several times, and so how could the first man be the right one? You've been warned endlessly that there will be temptations along the way. And that's without taking into account that he, too, will have no shortage of options.

Yes, it's all true. Statistically speaking, you're (far) more likely to break up with him than to love him till death do you part. If he doesn't call you back, then he wasn't worth it. He'll find someone he is more suited to. And so much the better—for you both.

But it's the exception that makes the rule—and isn't life the sum of these exceptions? You can never be absolutely sure (in love or, for that matter, in anything), and the perfect man doesn't exist: they all need to be wrong for the one to be right. Love is the only part of your life in which you truly have no choice.

The good news is that over the course of your various liaisons—and incidentally all your not-so-glorious moments—you have learned to truly know yourself, to be strong and independent, to get by on your own. And so you don't need anyone else to be happy. But you have to admit that, with him, it's better.

In Paris, like anywhere else, it's good to know how to look beyond your preconceptions, in order to become a girl in love.

A Woman's Real Assets

*Based on a fable by
psychiatrist Milton Erickson*

Milton Erickson (1901–1980) was by no means a Parisienne but a great American psychiatrist, specializing in human behavior, hypnosis, and family therapy as a way of treating neuroses.

A childhood experience proved to be especially seminal to his work: farmers were trying to get a young calf out of its stall, but it did not want to leave. The farmers tried pulling it out by its tail, to no avail: the calf pulled the other way and would not budge.

Suddenly, one of the farmers had an idea.

What they needed to do was pull the calf's tail in the other direction, toward the stall rather than away from it. The animal immediately changed its mind and ran out, leaving the stall of its own accord.

From this, Milton Erickson derived an important discovery about human psychology—we often get it all wrong, trying one thing exhaustedly when all it takes is doing the exact opposite to achieve the desired effect.

Here is the Parisienne's secret arsenal when she finds herself in a lovers' quarrel:

TEARS
Some women think that men are moved by their tears. Perhaps they still harbor the illusion that opening the floodgates used to work well on their parents.

If you believe that tears are a vibrant sign of your vulnerability, think again. Forget the notion that they are heart-wrenching in any way. Crying is not a weapon, it's little more than noise and needlessly wasted energy.

Unless you never cry.

In which case, the one time you do, you can be sure your tears will floor him.

But beware it's a one-trick pony. Pick your moment wisely, because you won't get a second shot.

JEALOUSY

Jealousy is a complete bore for all involved, regardless of whether you're on the giving or receiving end of it. It's a no-win game.

Instead of fanning the flames and causing a scene, retract your claws and nip the fantasy in the bud. You could say, "Not only is that woman beautiful, but she's such fun and clever too!" Acknowledging the fantasy is the surest way of extinguishing its spark.

If, however, the appeal lingers, if the situation becomes riskier than expected, invite your adversary to your home for dinner. Setting a fox among the geese will make it a gosling. Worst-case scenario, you'll have a new friend.

BELITTLEMENT

Belittling him to put him at your mercy—that's just wishful thinking. Telling him that he doesn't measure up to any old Joe picked up off the street is useless. Saying hurtful and disagreeable things won't make him change. It'll only make him run. Why would he stay with someone who clearly has such a low opinion of him? Instead, shower him with compliments. As his ego is being boosted by your flattery, he will want only one thing: to try to be more like the image you painted of him.

THE IN-LAWS

Don't ever speak ill of your in-laws. Tell him your mother-in-law is the ideal woman. He'll never get over it.

SULKING

In France, we have this very colorful expression for sulking in bed: *l'auberge du cul tourné—the inn of the turned ass.* In a nutshell, it means the only action your partner will get is a front-row viewing of your backside.

The problem with sulking is that it is an act of self-punishment. It's a waste of time that could be better spent channeling creative energy. Instead of sulking, play the role of the perfect woman—it is far more destabilizing. Be cheerful, bright, and sensual—anything but sullen. Once he realizes all that he stands to lose, an apology and mea culpa will come sooner than expected.

When you've made up, unmake the bed. Getting under the sheets rather than under each other's skin will heal both your wounds.

EMOTIONAL BLACKMAIL

Emotional blackmail will get you nowhere. As for threatening to commit suicide, no one will believe you'd actually go through with it. So forget about swallowing an entire bottle of homeopathic pills. The only thing you'd prove is that you're not a woman of your word.

Instead of threatening to disappear forever, disappear for real. Without a word, pick up your purse and keys and slam the door behind you. Go get some air. Whether it's for an hour or a week, put some distance between you. And silence (switch off your phone). Take a deep breath, and feel how good it is to be alive.

IN LOVE WITH LOVE

Imagine a scrap of wood and toss it into a frozen lake. Wait a while. Slowly, it will be coated in a thin layer of ice until it is transformed and sparkles as brightly as a diamond. This process is called *crystallization*. In his book *On Love,* the nineteenth-century French author Stendhal wrote that falling in love works much the same way. At first, the object of love appears to be absolutely perfect, even extraordinary. For Stendhal, the period of *crystallization* is fleeting, obsessional, and quixotic—a phase during which the object of affection is completely idealized. For most, this state passes soon enough, but not for the Parisienne. The Parisienne is in love with the *idea* of love. To a pathological degree. Her entire life revolves around the flutterings of her heart.

Crystallization is her personal form of madness and will make her do just about anything:

Write letters she will never send. ✻ **Spend a fortune on lingerie no one will ever see.** ✻ Fall for three men in the same week with equal intensity. ✻ **Cancel work meetings so she can wait for a phone call that may never come.** ✻ Dream up a life with someone who doesn't even know her name.

Voilà, the secret of the Parisienne, the reason for her flushed cheeks, her wistful smile. Her love of love. And even if the object of her affection changes from one day to the next, the feeling remains the same. She is incredibly faithful, just not to the same man.

A Mother's Advice on Love

She received these words of wisdom from her mother, and passed them on to us as soon as we could walk. They have reverberated throughout our lives first as stepping-stones, then as guides, and finally as mantras. And to be honest, we haven't always agreed with them. At times they've even annoyed us because they have derailed our plans. But then, as we grew up, we came to face the facts: Mother was right all along.

To be passed on, whether or not you have children:

* Always be prepared, he could be just around the corner.

* Love alone is not enough. You have to work at it.

* Age should never be an excuse to go to bed early.

* Be financially independent, so that you love only for love.

* When you no longer want to love each other, it's that you're still in love. When you still want to love each other, it's that you've fallen out of love.

* If he's the right horse, he'll come back at a gallop.

* Just because you have only one life doesn't mean you should be afraid of wasting it.

"The only beautiful eyes are those that look at you with tenderness."

—COCO CHANEL

A LITTLE EXTRA SOMETHING

"You're pregnant!" It's such great news! But in grammar as in life, the word "pregnant" is an adjective. It describes you, it doesn't define you.

You take advantage of your newfound cleavage to experiment with the décolleté: you are sexy.

You beam, you cry, you dissolve into hysterical laughter: you're a woman on the edge.

You buy things in extra-large at H&M rather than go to a maternity store: you have flair.

You don't think of yourself as the eighth wonder of the world: you are realistic.

You don't complain to your co-workers about your stretch marks: you are discreet.

You'd rather discuss the last film you saw, not Lamaze breathing: you are in tune with the times.

You live for moments of happiness so intense that you think you'll explode: you are a woman in love.

You don't discuss your fear of an episiotomy with your brother-in-law: you know your manners.

You don't believe that your belly entitles you to be high maintenance: you are a grown-up.

You don't share the photos from your last ultra-sound with your entire address book: you still have some secrets.

You don't plan a baby shower: you don't need to celebrate the fact that you had sex eight months ago.

You wear high heels until the day you walk into the delivery room: you never surrender.

You replace your Bloody Marys with Virgin Marys, but that's it: you're no saint.

You don't feel guilty because you missed your last birthing classes: you are a free woman.

You are not defined by this stage of your life. This is a period of growth. You are a pregnant woman, which means you are above all a woman. With a little extra something.

THE PARTY

It's 10:59 p.m.

When you finally turn off your computer your eyes are red from staring at the screen. Your colleagues left long ago. This is when you wish that someone were still around, a living soul to witness, or even just two hands to applaud, your long day's work. You slam the door and hop on your scooter. You need to be around people—anyone will do. You're off to join a flaky girlfriend at some random party. But hey, a party is still a party. At this unlikely hour, when you're craving company and a roll of the dice, anything will do the trick.

It is forty minutes later, and you and your plastic champagne flute have both lost their luster. You're staring at a bookshelf, trying to feign interest.

—So, how's that drink treating you, Zelda? Quite the party, huh?

Some brown-haired guy has come to badger you, obviously amused to see you stranded. You try to dodge the bullet and discourage him:

—Have you no one else to talk to . . . ?

—Oh, I do, but they're a lot less entertaining than you are. Watching a pretty girl alone at a party where she doesn't know a soul, kicking her heels in front of a pile of books at midnight—it doesn't get much better than that.

—Quite the smooth talker when you like someone, aren't you?

—Who says I like you?

This animal is cleverer than you thought. He's not wrong and you both know it, but you'd sooner stick to your guns and battle it out than admit defeat. But let's face it, you're here alone, desperately alone. The friend you were supposed to meet got lost along the way, which doesn't surprise you: in Paris, at night, it's every woman for herself.

You tell yourself that the best way to get this guy to leave you alone is probably to keep quiet. You turn and home in on the conversation between the two drunk girls next to you.

—Wait, I don't get it . . .

—I swear, he told me he was going to "bang me"!

—My goodness, they've all gone crazy . . .

—Yeah, but weirdly enough, it kind of turned me on.

You don't have time to dwell on this nocturnal poetry. The stubborn guy, sensing your distraction, gives it another shot.

—Are you always this boring or is it me?

You're about to brush him off once and for all, when you spot your infamous ex walking in. Clearly, this is your lucky night. Suddenly you feel the urge to look busy, to act like you find this conversation interesting. Time to reload.

—Let me get this straight, tough guy—did you come here to talk or to insult me?

He hesitates for a moment, scrutinizing you.

—All I'm trying to do is hit on a girl I like.

—See, told you you liked me.

He pulls himself together. Now you've got the upper hand. But your ex gives you a half wave from across the room (what a jerk) while his new girlfriend blatantly ignores you and continues mingling (what a bitch). In your unhappiness you tell yourself that despite everything, this guy next to you at least gets credit for masking your distress (what a trooper).

That's the moment another male nuisance decides to make his move. But you cut him off before he has a chance to utter a word:

—Not right now, please.

He leaves with his tail between his legs while the guy still standing next to you bursts out laughing. He didn't miss a second of your merciless putdown.

—You women crack me up! You all claim you're feminists who believe in gender equality, but when it comes to making the first move, you're all the same.

You bounce back, ready for the final battle.

—Listen, we don't know each other so I'm going to cut to the chase. You can't blame me for all the other times a woman has snubbed you.

He stares at you. There's a malicious twinkle in his eye.

—No, *you* listen to *me*. Let me explain what it really means to be a man. Maybe then you'll think twice the next time a guy risks his life by trying to talk to you. He's got to:

1. Know how to get rejected without taking it personally.

2. Rebound as if nothing happened.

3. Find something interesting to talk about even though he knows the woman in front of him is checking out some guy behind his shoulder. A guy she's most likely slept with but who doesn't seem to be fighting for her attention anymore.

4. Keep talking to her, without asking himself why the other guy isn't fighting to take his place.

5. And keep being a gentleman even after she insults another guy who had the sheer audacity to approach her.

At this point, you know he's played his cards right (and maybe you're even starting to like him).

He continues.

—And if you persevere, and this awful girl finally decides she
likes you, you'll have to deliver. The pressure will come down
on you and you'll need to get a hard-on. The little voice you
know all too well will wake up and say, "Go for it, it's your
turn to play. It's now or never!" And the little voice will never
shut up even after you've overcome your fear of failure. It will
yell even louder, "No, no! Not now, not yet, NO!" You'll hold
yourself back, you'll struggle, and then you'll finish your duty,
without honor or glory, hoping that the girl won't sulk after
the fact. That's it.

Suddenly you understand that this guy deserves a round of
applause. Or even just two enthusiastic hands, clapping to the
rhythm. Just like you did when you left the office alone that
night. We're all misunderstood heroes, overcoming perilous situ-
ations with no one there to give us a medal.

The guy looks at you. You smile at him. You light a cigarette and
pluck up your courage; you take a drag and feel your heart melt.

—Are you kidding me, I thought you quit smoking?!

You turn and see that your girlfriend has finally decided to show
up. The guy feels that he's unwanted and slips away with dignity.
You hesitate for a moment, before ditching your friend.

Nope, you won't be going to bed alone tonight.

AFTER-SEX LUNCH— HAPPY ENDING

You're lying next to each other, catching your breath. Alas—as you know by now, sex tires men out. You accept him as he is, in his sorry state. But then you have a brilliant idea. You escape quietly to the kitchen. You open the fridge, and bring out some cheese, eggs, a slice of ham. You prepare an omelet, beating the eggs and adding a pinch of salt and pepper and a dash of milk. As soon as the butter begins to sizzle in the pan, you pour in the mixture. You put some bread into the toaster and open a bottle of red wine. You hurry, he mustn't fall asleep. Next to the Comté and the ham, you set the toast, a glass of wine, and a steaming plate. In less than ten minutes, you're back in the bedroom.

You place the tray on the bed.

He opens his eyes slowly.

La vie est belle.

BEING NAKED

While the sight of bare breasts in the French media is rather common-place and long gone are the days when it shocked anyone, the Parisienne remains modest when it comes to her own nudity. Just because a Frenchman painted *The Origin of the World* some 150 years ago doesn't make it acceptable for us to prance around naked whenever we feel like it.

Nudity must be treated like an apparition. Like a game between lovers, it must never feel gratuitous or mundane, it must never be taken for granted. It should always be meaningful.

When you walk around naked, you're allowing yourself to be seen—and the person you're with should know it's intentional. You're creating excitement. Even if you're in a long-term relationship, don't slouch, hold your head up high. You've learned to know your body and you can accommodate its peculiarities.

You're a different woman when you're undressed: if you don't like your ass, walk sideways, your back to the wall, and show off your breasts. If your legs are too short or your thighs too wide, go on your tiptoes. If you don't like your breasts . . . do something about them, but in the meantime, cross your arms, and when in bed, opt for positions lying on your back.

In short, you're not a slave to the cult of the perfect body—so learn to make the best of what nature gave you.

GIRLS GANG

At first glance, one might think that Parisiennes don't get along with one another, because in theory, two of them in the same room is one too many. Often when they first meet, they size each other up, shooting daggers at each other, as though they were in some kind of modern Western. But this hostility never lasts long.

It's hard to say if it's strategy, common sense, or seasoned feminism at work, or if a real affinity exists between them, but the fact remains that Parisiennes often work best as a team. They like to form small but solid units in which the qualities of each complement the others so much that the group itself becomes even greater, more desirable and seductive.

As confident as she may be, the Parisienne understands that she needs other women in her life: the long-lost childhood friends she reconnects with years later; the high school friends who were there for all her firsts—French kiss, playing hooky, getting dissed, first time, morning-after pill—and then there are the friends for life, the ones she can always count on, the ones who find her on their doorstep, suitcase in hand, after she's been dumped. They'll get pregnant at the same time, perhaps because they can't actually have children with each other.

Without her girls gang, the Parisienne is incomplete.

THE ONE WHO
GOT AWAY

You've known this man for a long time.

You find him handsome. Funny. A bad boy and a ladies' man.

You've liked him from the moment you first laid eyes on him.

As for him—he adores you. You are the only woman who gets him, the only woman worthy of the name, the only one who could find favor in his eyes. In a nutshell, you are the only woman he loves—after his mother, of course.

In the best of all possible worlds, everything would be fine. But though this man loves you, adores you, he isn't in love.

As strange as it might seem—and in spite of your innumerable qualities—he'll never even contemplate sleeping with you. Let alone marry you. Or have children with you. Not even a kiss!

Your mother dreams of your marrying him (*"I'm sure he's just waiting for you to make up your mind"*). Your best friend suggests that you get him drunk so he'll lose his inhibitions (*"He's just shy!"*). Your neighbor advises you to stand naked in front of him and make a phone call (*"It's the best way to find out if he's gay"*).

But he's not shy, or bewitched, or gay. It's not that at all. Listen to these words of wisdom, because your Parisian friends will never let you live a lie: if nothing's happened yet, it's because *this man will never want you*. It's not fair, and there's no rational explanation for it. But that's the way it is. You're wasting your time. Get dressed and move on.

NOT A
WEDDING

Statistically speaking, Parisiennes don't often get married.
Even if they've been with the same person for many years, even if they
have children together.

Marriage isn't much of a tradition in the French capital as women
there would rather "feel free," "not sign a contract to prove their love,"
and "avoid having to lie when they swear they will be together forever."
Who can tell what will happen tomorrow?

Now that this disclaimer is out of the way, here's the truth: every
Parisienne dreams of her wedding. It's kept snug at the back of her
mind, an idea, a reverie, a project.

Here is, as strange as it may seem, the archetypal ideal of "the most
beautiful day of her life." Don't forget—these Parisiennes have strange
tastes. They devour oysters and escargots.

THE PROPOSAL

Frequently, she is the one to propose. Obviously, just like everyone else,
she wants this moment to be original and unique.

But she also doesn't want her future husband choking on a ring hidden inside a macaroon, so she favors a more direct approach.

—Remind me, what are your middle names?

—Marcel and Jean, after my grandfathers. Why?

—I'm at city hall right now. I'm booking a wedding date. You don't mind, do you?

THE WEDDING PLANNER

As a grown woman able to get dressed by herself; have children by herself; say *merde* to her parents; and handle illnesses, bosses, daily injustices, and a thousand other responsibilities by herself, the last thing she wants to deal with is a crazy, hysterical, and frustrated wedding planner trying to tell her how to organize her wedding.

—Darling, are you sure December twenty-seventh is a good date to get married?

—Yes! Our wedding will be the one fun evening we spend with your family during the Christmas holidays . . .

—Well, perhaps it's not such a bad idea.

THE BACHELORETTE PARTY

In French, we still refer to this as *l'enterrement de vie de jeune fille*—translated literally as "a maiden's funeral," except that a Parisienne hasn't been a maiden for quite some time. So it is out of the question to organize some sunny weekend at the beach, with initiation rites, photo ops, and limousines. Instead she'll invite only her closest friends—both men and women, because her best friend might be her ex—to a lovely old-school brasserie. There everyone will drink champagne as they eat their blood sausage (only AAAAA—see Fifteen Words You Need). *Basta.*

—Let's raise a glass to the future bride!

—Tchin-Tchin!

—Hey . . . why are you getting married anyway?

—Because in the event I want to get a divorce one day, it's a lot easier.

THE WEDDING DRESS

The poufy meringue look is out of the question. She will get married in either a black or navy blue tuxedo. Or in a vintage couture dress. Or else, in the middle of winter, in a gigantic white fur coat. She knows exactly what she wants, and certainly won't monopolize her friends' precious time by dragging them to every bridal shop in town.

—That one really suits you. Is it for a special occasion?

—Just for my wedding.

THE WEDDING RING

The Parisienne dreams of a simple ring, no diamonds, nothing flashy. A family ring with sentimental value will do just fine. Or a copper band, bought for a pittance on a road trip with her boyfriend. She doesn't want to encumber her silhouette with a heavy and expensive rock.

—You're not going to wear your wedding ring every day?

—Are you kidding? What next—I'll have to take my husband's name, too? Let's not get carried away here.

—So why are you getting married?

—I can't wait to be able to answer the phone and say, "Hold on, I'll get my husband."

THE WEDDING LOCATION

Paris, of course. First at the city hall in her arrondissement, and then at a place of worship, if she's religious. The champagne toast will take place at a little bistro that she knows well, on one of the capital's lovely squares. No castles in Lorraine or rented manors in Burgundy. At night, everyone will head over to her apartment, which will be full of white flowers for the occasion. Friends and friends of friends will joyously wreck the place in celebration. Sketches, songs, video projections, and other rituals are absolutely forbidden. That day, everything will be improvised—even the speeches.

THE GUESTS

She invites only people she wants to see—which comes down to no more than about twenty guests. First of all, she doesn't have the means to feed everyone, and doesn't see why she should ask her parents or in-laws to pay for a party. And so much the better, because that way she doesn't feel obliged to invite her in-laws *or* her parents. And as she hasn't even told them . . .

—You got married? I can't believe you didn't tell us!

—Did you invite your parents when you and dad got married?

—They had already passed away!

—You see, that's why I didn't invite you. You always bring everything back to your own suffering.

THE HONEYMOON

Instead of a traditional honeymoon trip, the Parisienne will treat herself to a night in one of Paris's most luxurious hotels—the Pavillon de la Reine, for example, overlooking the Place des Vosges. Her secret wedding dress is actually the silk lingerie she bought for herself. The next day she'll walk home barefoot, like a true Cinderella, hand in hand with her Prince Charming.

SEPARATE
BEDROOMS

Couples now often don't choose to sleep in separate bedrooms. A few decades ago, our grandparents still abided by this tradition: they slept separated by thick walls and a touch of modesty. When we were younger this habit seemed archaic, old-fashioned, and downright strange. But we've since grown up and made two discoveries: First, that a couple sometimes needs a little space. And also, that today's prohibitive rents keep us from resurrecting this two-bedroom idea. "Separate bedrooms" no longer means to create two distinct spaces for him and her in one apartment, but rather to sleep apart regularly enough in different locations that you start to miss each other. And so sometimes we force the situation. We take off to the countryside on a whim or stay later than expected at a girlfriend's house chatting the night away and then decide to stay over on the spur of the moment. Or we might even concoct a business trip, creating a work commitment that separates us for a while and then brings us closer together, an antidote to routine. All for the pleasure of that phone call and hearing him say, "It's cold, without you."

"*Trust firmly in your luck, cling to your happiness and dare to take risks. They will see you and learn to accept you.*"

—RENÉ CHAR, *THE DAWN-BREAKERS*

- DO YOU? LOVE me!

- YES.

- Truly??

- OF COURSE.

FOREVER?

YES *my Love.*

EVEN When I'm OLD,

and UGLY?

FAT

EVEN

WHEN YOU'RE OLD, FAT AND UGLY.

DIRTY LIAR.

5

PARISIAN TIPS

Spending Time
the Parisian Way

HOW TO SPEND A PARISIAN DAY

Greet the waiter in your local café with *la bise* on your way to work in the morning.

Don't eat breakfast.

Read the newspaper by yourself on your lunch break.

Listen to the radio in the kitchen while making dinner.

Drink at least one glass of red wine between 7:30 p.m. and 10:30 p.m.

Jot down in your notebook the charming turn of phrase you heard while doing your grocery shopping.

Always put on perfume before going out, especially on the nape of your neck and your wrists.

Never change your shoes—even if it means suffering on the Métro in five-inch heels.

Decide to rearrange your furniture.

Put it off till tomorrow.

Realize that, against all odds, you've fallen in love even though that's simply *impossible*.

Go to bed with all your jewelry on, but having taken all your makeup off.

HOW TO SPEND A PARISIAN WEEK

Travel to the provinces for work. Swear never to live there.

Watch an old film on the couch with your best friend, but never in bed. Parisians wouldn't dream of having TVs in their bedrooms.

Host a Parisian dinner party.

Talk to everyone in the same tone of voice, whether it's your parents, the taxi driver, your boss, a celebrity you met at a bar, or the newspaper vendor on the corner.

Have a Saturday night on a Wednesday.

Treat yourself to some flowers to brighten up your apartment.

Take up an artistic hobby: play in a rock band, sing in a baroque choir, enroll in a Portuguese pottery class, sign up for a writing workshop.

Cancel your gym session to have a drink with your friend who's just been dumped.

Decide it's great to get dumped, because falling in love again makes you lose your appetite, and in turn eat fewer calories—which defeats the need for that gym membership.

See your psychoanalyst.

Sell a pair of shoes on eBay to pay for aforementioned psychoanalyst.

Contemplate the Lacanian relationship between your Oedipus complex and the fact that you sold your shoes on eBay to pay for your psychoanalyst.

HOW TO SPEND A PARISIAN WEEKEND

Promise yourself you won't go out on Friday, so as to get a good night's rest.

Nevertheless, go for a drink after work, then get dragged to a restaurant, and end your night in a club, in spite of yourself.

Be thankful that you always wear nice lingerie—you never know what might happen.

Wake up on Saturday morning in bed with your best guy friend, before launching into a long discussion about the "stakes" and the "ins and outs," as well as the "subtext" of the situation.

Alternatively, wake up on Saturday morning in your building, looking out at the same view as from your apartment, but at a slightly lower angle. Realize you're in your downstairs neighbor's bed.

Eat croissants and buttered toast for breakfast—because it's Saturday morning and you burned enough calories last night, damn it.

Agree to (at least a little) exercise but only in "beautiful" surroundings: a run in a picturesque public park or a swim in a historically listed pool.

Go to the market on Sunday morning with your wicker basket. Prepare a delicious lunch with vegetables, fresh bread, and salted butter.

Take a nap on Sunday afternoon, because there's nothing better to do. Preferably at the same time as your children or your new lover.

Invite your friends over for dinner to stave off the Sunday evening blues.

If they don't come, eat a tartine of Camembert accompanied by a bottle of excellent Bordeaux—also to fight the Sunday blues.

Promise yourself you'll spend next weekend in the countryside.

Paris Cutouts

Always take a bit of Paris with you.

THE
ABC'S OF
CHEATING

Rule number one: DENY, DENY, DENY.

Don't feel guilty. This is about you, not *against* him.

What's good for you is good for your relationship: basically, you're just being a thoughtful girlfriend.

Your lover should not be part of your circle of friends: it's okay to cheat on your boyfriend, it's not okay to humiliate him. His honor matters just as much as your personal fulfillment.

Save your lover's number under "Private Number."

Better yet, save it under your best friend's name. (She's so needy . . .)

There is no such thing as a secret that stays a secret. The truth always comes out. Refer back to rule number one.

Protect yourself—against disease and love itself (which can also make you very sick).

Never complain to your lover about your boyfriend. Who wants to fool around with a woman who's dating a loser?

Keep things straight: don't treat your lover like a boyfriend.

Shake it up and spread the love: cheat on your lover with your boyfriend.

The Art of
Make-Believe

The secret to making a man know you need him:

Of course you can open a bottle of wine by yourself.

But let him do it. That's equality, too.

CLASSIC (AND FOOLPROOF) FRENCH RECIPES

A Parisienne loves her classics. But should her culinary skills fail her, she has a few tricks up her sleeve that she never shares with anyone.

CREPES

Crepes are a specialty in France's Brittany region, but the whole country makes them for their children on Shrove Tuesday. According to tradition, it's fun to flip them in the air, especially when they land on somebody's head and not in the pan.

You can find a variation with caramelized sugar and Grand Marnier in Parisian brasseries under the name Crêpes Suzette.

INGREDIENTS

1 cup flour
3 eggs
1 tablespoon vegetable (not olive) oil
3 tablespoons sugar (or vanilla sugar)
Pinch of salt
1 to 2 tablespoons water
2 cups milk
½ cup beer

Serves 4
Prep time: 10 minutes
Resting time: 1 hour
Cooking time: 4 minutes per crepe

Put the flour in a mixing bowl.

Trick number 1: *First sift the flour through a fine sieve or small mesh strainer. This will ensure that the batter doesn't turn lumpy.*

Make a well in the middle of the flour with your hand and add the eggs, oil, sugar, salt, and water. Mix thoroughly with a wooden spoon. Add the milk while stirring continuously until you have a smooth batter.

Trick number 2: *Add half a cup of beer to the batter. This gives the crepes a wonderfully light consistency. (The alcohol will evaporate during cooking.)*

Add the beer, stir, and cover the batter with a dishtowel. Leave to rest one hour.

Next, heat up a large sauté pan that you've greased with an oil-soaked paper towel. With a ladle, pour enough batter into the pan so that it spreads out evenly—it should be no thicker than a pinhead or a quarter. Cook for about 2 minutes, then flip. If you're feeling brave, try flipping it in the air with a flick of the wrist. Otherwise, use a spatula.

Trick number 3: *There's an old wives' tale that says if you hold a coin in one hand while cooking, it will bring prosperity to your household.*

It's ready! Eat the crepe folded into halves or quarters, sprinkled with sugar, or filled with jam, chestnut purée, whipped cream . . . Anything goes.

ILE FLOTTANTE (FLOATING ISLAND)

This dessert is a showstopper, easy to prepare, and *light*. It's the perfect way to end an otherwise copious dinner. Parisian bistros serve it with a drizzle of caramel and shaved almonds.

INGREDIENTS
1 vanilla bean
2 cups milk
6 eggs, separated
1½–2 cups sugar
1 teaspoon flour
Pinch of salt
Caramel sauce (jarred or homemade)

Serves 6 to 8 people
Prep time: 20 minutes
Cooking time: 15 minutes
Resting time: 10 minutes
Total: 45 minutes

Start by making crème anglaise: make a slit down the vanilla bean and add it to the milk. Bring the milk to a boil, remove from heat, and then remove the bean.

Trick number 1: *You can substitute vanilla extract for the bean. (The beans can be very expensive.)*

In a separate bowl, beat the egg yolks with 1½ cups of the sugar until the mixture is white and frothy. Add to the warm milk and return the mixture to the stove over low heat to thicken it.

Trick number 2: *Add a teaspoon of flour to the mixture to give it a nice thickness.*

Add the flour and stir continuously with a wooden spoon to prevent the mixture from boiling. After a few minutes, when the white froth on top has disappeared, remove from the heat. Place it in the refrigerator to cool while you prepare the islands.

In a large pot, bring 8 cups of water to a boil. In a medium bowl, beat the egg whites and a pinch of salt and slowly add 2 tablespoons of the sugar until stiff. Using two large spoons, delicately make the egg whites into balls and ladle them into the boiling water. Each island will take 1 to 2 minutes to cook. They are done once the whites are hardened, but make sure they stay moist. Then carefully scoop them out onto paper towels. Serve two or three islands per portion, in cups filled with crème anglaise, and cover them with caramel sauce.

Trick number 3: *If you're making your own caramel sauce, use five sugar cubes per tablespoon of water. Add a good splash of lemon juice. Make sure to watch the pan; when it begins to brown, add a few drops of vinegar so it doesn't burn.*

MAYONNAISE

Some people believe that to succeed in the art of mayonnaise, you need the stars to align . . . Whether or not that's true, homemade mayonnaise is a delicacy, a treat, to be savored with a simple hard-boiled egg, raw vegetables, or seafood.

INGREDIENTS
1 egg yolk
1 tablespoon strong mustard
Salt and freshly ground pepper
¼ cup vegetable oil
A drizzle of vinegar (or lemon juice)

Prep time: 10 minutes

In a large bowl, whisk together the egg yolk and mustard with a dash of salt and pepper. Add the oil in a drizzle while whisking constantly with an electric beater. In order to create an emulsion, this must be done slowly, so you can feel the concoction gradually thicken and blend. Finish by adding the vinegar or lemon juice. Feel free to flavor your mayonnaise with a dash of nutmeg, paprika, or even saffron.

Trick number 1: *Take the ingredients out of the fridge ahead of time so they warm up to room temperature.*

Trick number 2: *Mayonnaise can be kept for up to twenty-four hours in the refrigerator if covered with plastic wrap that "touches" the surface of the mayonnaise, but it doesn't keep any longer than that.*

VINAIGRETTE

So many recipes, so many variations: to each her own. Some people use old-fashioned grainy mustard, some like to add soy sauce, some throw in a pinch of sugar, and some put in chopped shallots, while others swear by balsamic vinegar. Whatever you choose, make sure to respect the order.

INGREDIENTS
Salt
1 part vinegar
1 part water
2 parts olive oil
Pepper

Mix all of the ingredients in a bowl.

The Trick: *Salt first, then vinegar, then water, then oil, and pepper last of all. In that order, without fail!*

Then, be creative and add whatever you feel like: parsley, chives, wasabi . . .

SETTING
THE TABLE

To set a table for a dinner party, there's no need to invest in a full set of china. However, anything "themed" (confetti, stones, fake flower petals, etc.) isn't welcome—it's not Mardi Gras. The table should reflect what you have, and not be overly coordinated. *Au contraire*, the china can be a mottled collection of your finds at flea markets.

Your glasses don't have to match either, but they should be clear (nothing colored) and should all have stems.

For the napkins, it is nice to use old embroidered white ones with a monogram. These cost next to nothing on eBay or can be taken from your grandmother's drawers.

There's no need to fold the napkins into complicated origami, simply place them on or alongside the plates.

At a Parisienne's table you will often find Laguiole folding knives, named after the French village where they are made. You can recognize them by the insect engraved on the handle.

It's probably better to cover your table unless it's a truly beautiful one. Old linen sheets make excellent tablecloths. They can be white or dyed.

On every table there is an open bottle of wine and a carafe of water (not a plastic bottle). If you don't have a salt shaker, put salt in two small dishes on either end of the table. The large wooden pepper grinders are called Rubirosas, after the Dominican playboy, and are the best.

ON YOUR
MANTELPIECE

* A postcard from a vacation. Whether a view of a deserted beach in Formentera or the Villa Malaparte in Capri.

* A newspaper clipping with a witty headline.

* A still from a cult film, torn out of a book or magazine.

* Photos. Photos of you now (though not too flattering—nothing that screams "look how beautiful I am"). A photo of you as a child, a blurred Polaroid shot, or a black-and-white strip from a photo booth.

* Movie tickets from films that you adored.

* Ticket stubs from art shows you loved.

* Invitations to your best friend's cocktail/premiere/engagement party.

* Mementos that make you smile (concert tickets, postcards gleaned from here and there).

* Your old ID card or first driver's license.

* A quote, a poem, a handwritten letter that moves you.

* An old black-and-white photo that you found in an antiques store or that was in your family.

* Seashells collected from here and there.

* Objects from your life that are always with you and give you pleasure whenever you look at them because they tell your story.

Being a feminist and appreciating gallantry are not necessarily incompatible—on the contrary. Making an effort, being attentive: it doesn't take much and yet it makes a world of difference. What a joy to find some grace and courtesy in this world of brutes. When you encourage his chivalry, a man becomes more a man, a woman more a woman.

And so, it's only normal that:

He hold the door for you.

He carry your suitcases and your shopping—a woman only ever carries her handbag.

He pour your wine; you should never have to touch the bottle. It suits him—that way you'll get drunk faster.

He take you home and wait for you to close the front door. Even if he tried to come up and you didn't let him. Making him wait—a little—never did anyone any harm.

LIGHTEN UP

reating the right mood in your apartment is more important than buying the right sofa or the latest shade of paint from Farrow & Ball. In fact, the decoration and life of your home should be organized around natural light. It is daylight that dictates the layout of your apartment and regulates its very heartbeat.

Think of lighting the way you do your makeup. Keep it mellow to soften the contours. Never have anything neon, unless it is part of a decorative piece. The aim is to create a warm and romantic atmosphere by using several sources of light, creating different moods for different rooms.

The kitchen: this is a strategic room, as it's where the Parisienne holds court. If you have enough space, create two different vibes: on one side the dining area, with soft lighting to inspire discussion and seduction; on the other side your worktop, with more direct light to prepare your roast lamb without cutting your finger.

The living room: make sure you accentuate the corners in a room, to open up the space. Use smaller lamps instead of a massive ceiling light, unless, of course, you've inherited a spectacular chandelier from your grandmother in which you can then put low-wattage lightbulbs. You can also keep a few candles here and there, but never on a low table: light from below only accentuates the bags under your eyes, and the shadow of your nose will give you a mustache.

The bedroom: keep the light low. Forget about the boring old lamp that draws attention to curves and cellulite. The only sources of light here should be the one in your closet and your reading lamp, which is never too harsh as it would only damage your eyes.

The bathroom is your best friend. Don't let it demoralize you! Choose a flattering light—even if it cheats a little—to make you feel good about yourself.

PLAYDATE

There are no casinos in Paris—gambling is illegal. But this hasn't stopped the Parisian tradition of playing games. Games are usually played around a table, during a dinner party or over drinks with friends (the more, the merrier).

INSTRUCTIONS

"Never Have I Ever" (the French way)

> **Number of players: 2 minimum**
> **Objects needed: full glasses, to consume in moderation or liberally**
>
> The first player starts by admitting something she has never done, for example, "Never have I ever had sex with a stranger." If the statement is true, she does nothing. If the statement is false, she takes a sip (of water, *bien sûr!*) to confess her lie. All other players must also answer and drink accordingly.
>
> You then move on to the next person, whose turn it is to admit "Never Have I Ever . . . ," and so on.
>
> Things tend to heat up pretty quickly.

"The Book Game"

Number of players: 2 minimum
Objects needed: a book

This is a so-called fortune-telling game.

Take a random book off the shelf, either fiction or nonfiction. Player 1 gets up and asks Player 2 to ask a question about her own life, as if addressing a fortune-teller. Then Player 1 asks Player 2 to choose from either the front or the back.

If she chooses from the front, Player 1 flicks through the pages of the book, starting from the front, until the other tells her to stop.

Next, Player 2 must choose right or left, which dictates which page will be read from.

And then Player 2 chooses a line number between 1 and 30. If she picks 14, Player 1 reads aloud the fourteenth line on the page.

This line is supposed to answer the question posed—often prophetic, it can then be analyzed by all the other players, before moving on to the next person.

"The Dictionary Game"

Number of players: 4 minimum
Objects needed: a dictionary, paper, pens

Player 1 chooses an obscure word in the dictionary that she believes no one will know the meaning of.

After spelling it out, the other players must then invent and write down, in dictionary jargon, a definition for this word. Player 1 writes down the real definition and then collects everyone else's, making sure not to let the other players know who wrote what.

Player 1 then reads out all the definitions, including the real one. Each player then votes for the definition they believe to be the most credible.

Those who guess correctly win a point. Those who write such a convincing definition that others vote for it win two points. The winner is the player with the most points at the end of the game.

"The Novel Game"

Number of players: 4 minimum
Objects needed: paper, pens, several novels

Following the same format as the Dictionary Game, this is played with novels.

One player reads the first line of the novel, and the others must invent the last line.

Little Big Treats

The Parisienne spends the same way she diets—the stricter she is with herself, the more likely she is to slip up. And that is when she decides to make a well-earned exception, convinced that she urgently needs one of the following:

* A bouquet of white lilies, just because. She loves treating herself to flowers.

* A first edition of a classic. It's the same story as in the more recent edition, but somehow the pleasure of reading it is not the same at all.

* A dish of sea urchins. They cost nothing in the South of France but are horribly expensive in Paris, which gives them an added taste of their own.

* A pair of oversized sunglasses to hide her tired eyes the morning after.

* An aromatherapy massage. But this isn't *really* a luxury, it's an investment in her well-being.

* That rare vintage piece she found on eBay and which she simply cannot live without.

* A romantic night at a hotel. Love is priceless.

* A nice candle, so she can feel the extravagance of a hotel at home—especially since a hotel is often beyond her means.

* A lacy lingerie set. On second thought, maybe just the bra. She'll figure out the bottom later.

Sunday Recipes

Parisians love to go to outdoor markets on the weekend, to find fresh produce that has undergone as little transformation as possible. Here are some easy, light, and delicious recipes.

These are quite simple recipes for Sundays—as you have plenty of things to do, you don't want to spend too much time in the kitchen!

FOR A SPRING SUNDAY /
ASPARAGUS WITH PARMESAN

Fresh asparagus, approximately 4 stalks per person
Olive oil, for drizzling
Juice of 1 lemon (optional)
Freshly shaved Parmesan
Salt and freshly ground pepper, to taste

Prep time: 5 minutes
Cooking time: 15 minutes

· Preheat the oven to 425°F.
· Trim the asparagus. Place on a baking sheet covered with aluminum foil and drizzle with the olive oil. Cook for 15 minutes in the hot oven. Soak up the oil with paper towels. Squeeze the lemon juice over the dish, if using. Sprinkle with the shaved Parmesan. Season with salt and pepper. Serve warm.

FOR A SUMMER SUNDAY / EGGPLANT CAVIAR

Serve as a dip or with a meat dish.

A drizzle of olive oil, plus more for greasing the pan
2 fleshy, large eggplants
½ shallot, minced
2 tablespoons of fresh lemon juice
½ teaspoon salt
Freshly ground pepper (4 turns of the mill)

Serves 4
Prep time: 5 minutes
Cooking time: 25 minutes

· Preheat the oven to 400°F.
· Grease a roasting pan with olive oil. Place the whole eggplants in the pan and bake for 25 minutes. They are done when they are swollen and soft.
· Remove the eggplants from the oven and let cool.
· Halve the eggplants and remove the pulp using a spoon. Place the pulp in a bowl and add the shallot. Add the drizzle of olive oil and the lemon juice and with a wooden spoon mix until the eggplant has absorbed all the oil and you have a smooth puree. Add the salt and pepper.

FOR AN AUTUMN SUNDAY / BAKED APPLE

This dish makes an excellent side dish (for meat or blood sausage).

If you want to serve it for dessert, prior to baking, fill the cored apple with a mixture of lemon juice and honey. Bake as before. While the apples are still warm, sprinkle with powdered sugar so that the sugar caramelizes. Serve warm, with or without ice cream or crème fraîche.

1 apple per person, preferably Renatta from Canada or Belle de
  Boscop varieties

Prep time: 5 minutes
Cooking time: 30 minutes

· Preheat the oven to 400° F.

· Rinse and core the apples. Place them in a baking pan, add a little
  bit of water, so the apples don't stick, and slide into the oven. When
  the skin begins to crackle and the flesh softens (approximately
  30 minutes, although it depends a bit on the size of the apples),
  take the apples out of the oven and serve them immediately.

FOR A WINTER SUNDAY / PEA AND CARROT SOUP

1 medium can of peas and carrots
Wasabi

Serves 6
Prep time: 5 minutes
Cooking time: 10 minutes

· Separate the carrots from the peas. Blend the carrots into a puree.

· Blend the peas together with the water from the can, into a soup.

· Heat them both, separately.

· Pour the carrot puree into the middle of a wide, shallow bowl, like
  an island.

· Then pour in the pea soup, all around the island.

· Make little wasabi balls, in the shape of peas, and arrange them
  around the rim of the bowl.

Ancestral Tips (We Never Forget Our Roots)

Paris is a land of exile and of providence, a veritable melting pot. If you go back to their family trees, most Parisiennes originally come from somewhere else. You'll discover flavors and scents from Brittany or Oran, and echoes from the Far East or darkest Africa—the fruit of successive waves of immigration that enrich and enliven the city.

Their families pass down advice from one generation to the next, secrets murmured in one another's ears. Whether beauty tips, recipes, or housekeeping notes, the Parisienne loves to draw on country wisdom that reminds her she is more than a rose that grew from concrete.

* Throw coffee grounds down the drain, never in the trash. They help degrease the plumbing and remove bad smells.

* Aspirin in the water makes your roses live a little longer.

* New shoes can be slippery. Catwalk pros cut up the soles with a knife—but rubbing them with half a raw potato works just as well.

* To give your hair that extra shine, use half a cup of white wine vinegar—simply pour it over your hair and rinse.

* Your skin, hair, and nails all love beer. Not the kind you drink—that gives you a belly—but instead beer in the form of brewer's yeast. Sprinkle it on salads, steak, vegetables. It's an excellent alternative to salt.

* Rum, honey, two egg yolks, and the juice of a lemon: not a recipe for baba au rhum, but just what you need for a restorative hair mask.

* Keep a pumice stone in your bathroom. Scrub your feet at least once a week to ensure they are always soft.

* In the baby section at the drugstore you can find sweet almond oil for next to nothing. Once you start using it, you'll never look back: it's a great hand and body moisturizer.

* At the end of your shower, spray your breasts with cold water.

* Before throwing out a juiced lemon, rub it on your fingernails— it'll strengthen and brighten them.

* Once a week, brush your teeth with baking soda—it's a natural whitener.

* Newspapers are perfect rags for cleaning windows, and they're more eco-friendly than paper towels.

WHEN YOU WATCH THESE FILMS, YOU'RE IN PARIS

Depending on Your Mood

If you have any doubts that Frenchwomen talk only about sex (even with their parents) and wander through the capital on the verge of breaking up with an American boyfriend, consider **2 Days in Paris**, written, directed by, and starring Julie Delpy. Yes, Parisian women are all totally crazy. (But to that extent, really?)

You've lost count of the number of times you've seen Vincente Minnelli's **An American in Paris** because you love musicals. Here's one that retraces the follies of young love today. Brace yourself. Impossible not to drool when confronted by handsome Louis Garrel in **Love Songs**, directed by Christophe Honoré.

Lose yourself in a black-and-white Paris during the aftermath of May 1968, when the main topic, after politics, was of course love. Its ups and downs, its crises, its joys. A couple makes up and breaks up in **The Regular Lovers**, directed by Philippe Garrel.

You're in love with a co-worker—but not any old co-worker. Not only is he your intern, he's just been released from prison. It seems that in Paris, any love is possible: **Read My Lips**, directed by Jacques Audiard.

To follow the life of a group of high school kids for a period of about fifteen years, and experience the fights, the backstabbing, the drugs, and the end of the idealistic seventies, go back to the **Good Old Daze**, directed by Cédric Klapisch. Because we've also all once been in love with our language assistant . . .

Keep track of the meanderings of a writer—a womanizer and a schmoozer—who decides to turn his life into a novel. In the smoky cafés of Paris, he chooses his prey, the young woman of the title, **La Discrète**, directed by Christian Vincent. Delight in this exposé of pure literary and cinematic perversity.

You'll fall in love with these two brothers—wonderful losers, fast-talkers, and revelers—who are the prototype of the Parisian male: irresistible and elusive. Yes, we live in the world of **Love Without Pity**, directed by Eric Rochant.

Obviously the most Parisienne of all French actresses is Catherine Deneuve. If you want to discover a dark chapter in Paris's history, the German occupation during World War II, don't miss **The Last Metro**, directed by François Truffaut.

To laugh affectionately at *l'esprit français* in all its glory, with men who love women who love men who cheat on their women, and if you also want to discover the Place de la Concorde and Paris's 16th arrondissement in the 1960s, watch **An Elephant Can Be Extremely Deceptive**, directed by Yves Robert.

If you're contemplating your empty fridge and the last remaining stick of butter, dance the **Last Tango in Paris**, directed by Bernardo Bertolucci. (Only if you are of age and not vulnerable.) With Marlon Brando, there's no turning back . . .

If you're torn between your husband and your lover, do as Romy Schneider does and make them become friends. **César and Rosalie**, directed by Claude Sautet, provides a French take on the idea of ménage à trois.

Who does Jean Seberg fall in love with while selling her *Herald Tribune*s on the Champs-Élysées? To find out, sit yourself in front of **Breathless** by Jean-Luc Godard. It also happens to be the greatest film of the famous New Wave.

If you sometimes imagine yourself walking alone in the streets of Paris in a perfectly tailored suit; if you love the city at night, its glowing sidewalks and yellow streetlights; if you tremble listening to the sounds of Miles Davis; if you have a lover who just did something really stupid: you are Jeanne Moreau, directed by Louis Malle in **Elevator to the Gallows**.

You want to explore the infamous Paris of the 1930s: let yourself be guided along the twists and turns of the Canal Saint-Martin and watch **Hôtel du Nord**, directed by Marcel Carné. Prepare your tissues for this black-and-white classic.

_Do you know **WHO** that is?

_OBVIOUSLY.

_She's **GORGEOUS** Don't you think?

_YES AND SHE KNOWS IT.

She's an ACTRESS AN *OUT OF WORK* ACTRESS. I'm invited to her **PARTY** on saturday night.

-OH...

Can I come?

"When you work to please others you can't succeed,
but the things you do to satisfy yourself stand a
chance of catching someone's interest."

—MARCEL PROUST, *PASTICHES ET MÉLANGES*

WHAT WE HAVE IN COMMON

FRENCH WORDS USED IN ENGLISH

adieu * à la carte * à la mode * à propos * Art Deco * *au naturel* * avant-garde * bon appétit * bourgeois * brunette * carte blanche * c'est la vie * *chaud-froid* * cherchez la femme * chic * cliché * coquette * *coup de foudre* * crème brûlée * crème de la crème * cuisine * cul de sac * debutante * décolleté * encore * ennui * faux pas * femme fatale * fiancé/fiancée * film noir * foie gras * haute couture * hors d'oeuvre * je ne sais quoi * joie de vivre * lingerie * Mardi Gras * ménage à trois * negligee * nouvelle vague * Oh la la! * papier-mâché * petite * prêt-à-porter * protégée * raison d'être * rendezvous * RSVP * sabotage * sangfroid * sans * savoir faire * *savoir-vivre* * souvenir * tête-à-tête * touché * tour de force * trompe l'oeil * vis-à-vis * voilà * *Voulez-vous coucher avec moi ce soir?* * *zut alors*

ENGLISH WORDS USED IN FRENCH

aftershave * babysitter * best seller * blackout * boom *
boss * brainstorming * break * briefing * business *
camping * casting * checkup * chewing gum * clash *
coach * comeback * cool * crash * design * discount *
dry martini * duty-free * escalator * fair play * fast food *
has-been * hobby * holdup * in/out * interview * kidnapping
* leader * lifting * lobby * look * must-have * nerd *
nonstop * one-man show * overbooking * overdose *
pacemaker * package * parking * penalty * planning * pole
position * pool * punk * puzzle * racket * remake * rock *
royalties * rush * scoop * self-control * sexy * shopping *
show * skateboard * skinhead * sponsor * stress * striptease *
talk show * timing * underground * weekend

Fifteen Words You Need

AAAAA

Parisians (and, more generally, the French) are keen lovers of what might at first glance appear to be very disgusting delicacies. Food that resembles things that we shall refrain from naming here, out of respect for common decency. The andouillette is a perfect example: made from a pig's digestive tract, which constitutes the andouillette's skin, it resembles a big fat sausage. It is a mix of veal and pork, seasoned with spices and wine. A delectable dish, you'll often find it preceded by the label "AAAAA," which stands for Association Amicale des Amateurs d'Andouillette Authentique (Friendly Association of Lovers of Authentic Andouillette). Dig in, mouth open wide (but eyes shut tight)—you won't regret it.

LA BISE

The French do *la bise* when saying hello and good-bye. That is to say they kiss, but not just any which way. To properly do *la bise,* both parties lean in so that only their cheeks graze, while making a kissing sound with their mouths; then this is repeated on the other side. Depending on where you are in France, the number of these kisses may vary. Whereas people in the South of France give four kisses, the Bretons stop at three. In Paris, you never do more than two. Note: one should never attempt to hug a Parisian. *La bise* may bring faces together, but bodies must stay apart.

CARNET

The Parisienne doesn't keep a diary nor does she confide her innermost thoughts to an imaginary friend. Someone always ends up reading your diary and that someone is often the person you'd most likely want to keep it hidden from. However, every Parisienne has a notebook in her purse, preferably a black Moleskine, in which she's constantly jotting down all sorts of things. Thoughts that cross her mind, a quote from a book that she liked, a to-do list, her favorite words, the lyrics of a song she wants to look up, the cell phone number of the guy she just met at a café, the previous night's dream that suddenly came back to her . . .

CAMEMBERT

It's a cliché but it's true: all Parisians eat cheese. Whatever the time of day. Some like to start the morning with a piece of Gruyère, some enjoy a slice of toast topped with goat cheese as a mid-afternoon snack, while others consider Camembert with a glass of red wine as the perfect nightcap after an evening out at a club. But beware: cheese, especially Camembert, is an art of its own. It's best to buy cheese from a cheese shop. But this is what even the biggest Parisian snobs will do: they'll buy all their cheese at the best cheese shop in Paris, *except* for the Camembert, which they'll buy at the supermarket. Preferably the Lepetit brand. Camembert has to be eaten runny, with the creamy heart oozing out of the rind. If not: don't even consider it.

LA PROVINCE

France can be separated into two geographical categories: Paris, and the provinces. What makes up the provinces? Anywhere that's not Paris.

PISCINE

Parisians often drink champagne. They know that this bitter, bubbly beverage can be the enemy of social events, especially when paired with petits fours (eaten to excess to stave off hunger)—and can cause what is known as "sewer breath." So Parisians invented the concept of a *piscine,* a swimming pool, which involves drowning a few ice cubes in your champagne. This reduces heartburn and eliminates the bad breath. And best of all, this drink is considered sacrilege by most "normal" people and thus flatters the snobbery of Parisians, who love to be known for their bad manners.

VIN ROUGE

There is no such thing as a French person who doesn't drink red wine. And, of course, the Parisienne has her own way of doing it. First of all—and this is very important—she chooses a favorite grape. She must be able to say, "I drink only Bordeaux, preferably Saint-Émilion" or, "You'll never catch me drinking a Côtes du Rhône!" She would never follow the rituals of a wine taster: the swirling, the sniffing, her nose deep inside the glass, followed by a series of gargling noises most commonly heard at a dentist's office. The Parisienne believes she was born with a "nose" or a "palate" and doesn't need to do anything to pretend to be an expert.

SAMEDI SOIR

The true Parisienne never goes out on Saturday night when the city's restaurants and nightclubs are overrun by drunk out-of-towners and students. Nothing significant would ever be scheduled for a Saturday, so there's no chance she might miss out on something. On Saturday night, the Parisienne stays home and hosts intimate dinner parties. Once a month, she might go out for a cultural event: the theater or the opera, an evening at a museum, or a recently restored classic film at the local cinema. It is absolutely unthinkable to organize a party on a Saturday night, unless it happens to be the day on which your birthday falls.

PSYCHANALYSTE

Most Parisians have a *psychanalyste* and can talk about it at great length. Those who don't are often "radically against it" and believe that neuroses are essential to the creative spirit. Either way, they all have a strong opinion about what one should and shouldn't do. That is, is it better to see a man or a woman, depending on whether you're a man or a woman? Is it preferable to see a Lacanian, a Freudian, or a Jungian? Is it necessary to pay for missed appointments or appointments scheduled on national holidays? However, Parisians will never divulge the details of their analysis, in the same way that they won't tell you about their dreams—one should never talk too much about oneself.

BOIRE UN VERRE

Parisians love to go for a drink, which is similar to getting coffee, but takes place strictly after 6:00 p.m. Paris is a city filled with bistros and cafés, where you can while away the hours chatting. To invite someone out for a drink is to informally ask him or her to hang out with you while drinking alcohol. There doesn't need to be a reason. It can last from one to two hours, during which any number of different things can be discussed, from the most intimate (your childhood traumas) to the most mundane (the weather). It is perfectly pleasant and is not a big commitment.

SOUS-TEXTE

The Parisienne spends much of her time analyzing the subtext: the true meaning behind people's words. This can lead to irrational discussions about "what did he *really* mean when he said that?" or "what was my mother-in-law trying to tell me when she gave me that gift?" or "was that just a Freudian slip or . . . ," etc.,

etc., etc. The Parisienne believes that she can read other people's minds better than anyone. She spends hours dissecting and pulling apart the words and acts of those around her, until everyone (herself included) is utterly exhausted.

CROISSANTS

Like Camembert, this cliché also happens to be true. The Parisienne loves to eat those crescent-shaped pastries that ooze butter and leave tiny flakes all over your face, clothes, and sheets. She eats them on Sunday mornings with her children. She eats them on Monday mornings before a stressful day at work. She eats them on vacation because without them it wouldn't be a vacation. And why doesn't she get fat from eating all these croissants? Because she's decided that she has the *right* to eat croissants without anyone giving her shit about how many calories they contain. *Merde alors!*

THÉÂTRE

It is astonishing how many theaters there are in the French capital. Every night, hundreds, even thousands, of Parisians settle into red-velvet-draped rooms and uncomfortable seats to watch a classic at the Comédie Française or to catch a new comedian at a tiny venue in northern Paris. As with most large cities, Paris attracts its fair share of actors trying their luck. At least two or three times a year, a friend will drag the Parisienne to sit through her latest show in some trendy basement in a suburb. *What a nightmare*. As for the older Parisienne, she has season tickets to the national theaters to see the latest productions. It's a habit that comes with age—in fact, that's how she can tell she's gotten old.

MARCHÉ

Each Parisian neighborhood has its own market. Some markets are daily, some can be covered, but the majority take place outdoors, twice a week, on a square. Parisians love going to the market. That's where they find vegetables that still have soil on them, and snails hidden in the lettuce. They love to chat with the vendors and show that they are regulars. Depending on the neighborhood, markets can either be a total rip-off or a great deal. To go to a market, dress casually and carry a large basket over your shoulder. It is even acceptable to bring one of those shopping carts grandmothers use, and let your baguette stick out of it. Some markets have their own specialties. It's also a great time to get to know the people in your neighborhood and grab a quick drink—*boire un verre*—before heading home to prepare lunch. Market days are a joyous time, often reminiscent of one's childhood.

PLOUC

Pronounced {plūk}, refers to any attitude considered common, charmless, even vulgar, from the point of view of the Parisienne. It's not a question of merit or social class: the first lady of France can be considered *plouc* if, for example, she calls her husband by his nickname in public.

ADDRESS BOOK

To truly live in your city, you need to know yourself well. Which means knowing your every need, desire, and problem, so that you can address them.

Every place has its function. You wouldn't take your great-aunt for lunch to the same place you take your lover.

You too can find:

* YOUR UNEXPECTED REFUGE

Somewhere slightly offbeat and a little strange, where you can wander when you need to forget the weight of your daily grind. A voyage through time.

Galerie de Paléontologie et d'Anatomie Comparée
2, rue Buffon, 75005 Paris
Museum

* THE END OF THE NIGHT

Legendary and old-fashioned, this restaurant is open at all hours. Actors rush here the minute they come off the stage and lovers can be seen gorging in the middle of the night.

A la Cloche d'or
3, rue Mansart, 75009 Paris
www.alaclochedor.com
Restaurant

✳ A DARK PLACE

To steal a first kiss, nothing beats the half-shadows of a giant aquarium.

L'Aquarium de Paris
5, avenue Albert de Mun, 75016 Paris
www.cineaqua.com
Aquarium

✳ YOUR MEETING ROOM

A neutral and chic Japanese tea salon for organizing a work appointment at the last minute.

Toraya—Salon de Thé
10, rue Saint-Florentin, 75001 Paris
Restaurant/Tea House

✳ A WALK IN THE CITY

Always know a place in the city that is bursting with history, where you can organize a picnic on nice days or go for a romantic stroll.

Les Arènes de Lutèce
47–59, rue Monge, 75005 Paris
Monument

✳ VEGGIES

A vegetarian restaurant because, no matter where you live in the world, you always have a friend from L.A. visiting. And just because you love a medium-rare steak doesn't mean you should ignore other people's preferences.

Tuck Shop
13, rue Lucien Sampaix, 75010 Paris
www.facebook.com/tuckshopparis
Restaurant

✳ PARISIAN CLOTHES

The store where shirts, dresses, and jackets instantly transform you into a native Parisienne. Indefinable, chic, and poetic.

Thomsen-Paris
98, rue de Turenne, 75003 Paris
www.thomsen-paris.com
Fashion

✳ HOME COOKING

A place where you rediscover your grandmother's cooking. For the past twenty years, this has been one of Paris's best-kept secrets, with its roasted vegetables *à l'ancienne,* steamed fish, and traditional meringues. To dine here is to get an education in good taste.

Pétrelle
34, rue Pétrelle, 75009 Paris
www.petrelle.fr
Restaurant

✳ MEDICINAL HERBS

If there's a waiting list of a few weeks for an appointment with your naturopath, then it's time to check out this little shop. You'll be given a quick, efficient, and free diagnosis. Treat yourself to a selection of purifying, antioxidant, and stimulating plants.

Herboristerie du Palais Royal, Michel Pierre
11, rue des Petits Champs, 75001 Paris
www.herboristerie.com
Health store

* A BIRTHDAY

This is where to order the best cake because you should never feel guilty about your parenting skills (and as far as we can remember, our mothers never slaved away in the kitchen for six hours to make a birthday cake).

Chez Bogato
7, rue Liancourt, 75014 Paris
www.chezbogato.fr
Bakery

* SMART DATE

A painting in front of which you arrange to meet your date so that he knows your true intentions. For example, *Liberty Leading the People* by Delacroix: a woman not afraid to show her breasts.

Musée du Louvre
75001 Paris
louvre.fr
Museum

* BRIGHT AND EARLY

The most beautiful place in the city to have breakfast. It's always good to begin the day with a blaze of glory. What's more, it's right next to the train station should you suddenly feel an overwhelming desire to get away.

Le Train Bleu
Gare de Lyon
Place Louis-Armand, 75012 Paris
le-train-bleu.com
Restaurant

* L'ORIGINE DU MONDE

A city square that is actually a triangle, because it's very erotic to kiss in a place that resembles the female sex.

Place Dauphine, 75001 Paris
Monument

* NIGHT OUT

A hotel restaurant where you can spend a lovely evening having dinner—with a bar where you can even make new friends if your date bores you.

Hôtel Amour
8, rue Navarin, 75009 Paris
hotelamourparis.fr
Hotel

* A HOTEL WITH A CAPITAL H

A boutique hotel nestled in the heart of Montmartre where you can have lunch away from prying eyes, in your own private garden.

L'Hôtel Particulier
23, avenue Junot, 75018 Paris
hotel-particulier-montmarte.com
Hotel

* WHEN YOU'RE FEELING DOWN

The bar of a luxury hotel where you can have a beer with your broken-hearted best friend. Because if you can't afford a room, you can at least indulge her with this.

English Bar at the Hôtel Raphaël
17, avenue Kléber, 75116 Paris
Hotel Bar

✳ THE MOST BEAUTIFUL OFFICE IN PARIS

A historic library where you can spend all day preparing for an exam, writing, and feeling inspired.

Bibliothèque Mazarine
23, quai de Conti, 75006 Paris
bibliotheque-mazarine.fr
Library

✳ AS PRETTY AS A POSTCARD

A neighborhood patisserie where you'll run into students from the Sorbonne and their professors and where you can eat comfort food on the go or drink a delicious hot chocolate.

Pâtisserie Viennoise
8, rue de l'École de Médecine, 75006 Paris
Bistro

✳ A GARDEN IN THE CITY

To have tea with your mother or your best friend. The garden is so lovely that you're well within your rights to pretend you're a heroine in a Jane Austen novel.

Musée de la Vie Romantique
16, rue Chaptal, 75009 Paris
Museum/Tea House

✳ A HANGOVER

Your go-to morning-after spot to eat a delicious cheeseburger or put yourself back together with a Bloody Mary.

Joe Allen
30, rue Pierre Lescot, 75001 Paris
Restaurant

* CINEMA PARADISO

The tiny movie theater where you feel at home, particularly on a Sunday evening when you want to watch an old Italian classic.

Le Reflet Médicis
3, rue Champollion, 75005 Paris
Movie Theater

* PERFECT PRESENTS

When you're short on time and ideas, here's a list of stores where you're always sure to find a gift that will make someone happy. Listed in order from the most affordable to the most expensive.

La Hune
6–18, rue de l'Abbaye, 75006 Paris
Bookstore

La Boutique de Louise
32, rue du Dragon, 75006 Paris
Jewelry/Home Decor

Cire Trudon
78, rue de Seine, 75006 Paris
Candles

7 L
7, rue de Lille, 75007 Paris
Fine Books

Merci
111, boulevard Beaumarchais, 75003 Paris
Concept Store

Astier de Villatte
173, rue Saint-Honoré, 75001 Paris
Home Decor

✳ VINTAGE FINDS

Even if you come away empty-handed, you'll have the satisfaction of having traveled through time and space. What's more, you'll feel like you've had a good workout after all that bargain-hunting.

Marché aux Puces de Clignancourt
Porte de Clignancourt, 75018 Paris
Flea Market

✳ AN IMPROMPTU DINNER PARTY

Your local deli that is open late on evenings and weekends, where you can always find good wine, cheese, fresh eggs, charcuterie, and home-made chocolates. In short, where you go when you invite friends over for dinner at the last minute.

Julhès
54, rue du Faubourg Saint-Denis, 75010 Paris
Grocery

✳ YOUR HQ

A café that is an extension of your living room and your office at the same time. You greet the owner, plug in your laptop, order a lemonade, and ask them to lower the music . . . and naturally the food is simple and delicious.

Restaurant Marcel
1, villa Léandre, 75018 Paris
Café/Bistro

✳ A ROYAL AFFAIR

A terrace where you feel like a queen. Yes, you'll pay more for your coffee for the privilege, but there's no view like this anywhere else in the world—and that's priceless.

Le Café Marly
93, rue de Rivoli, 75001 Paris
Café/Restaurant

✳ OFF THE BEATEN PATH

A dive of a bar where anything is possible. The temperature rises as soon as you walk through the door and the dark corners spark your imagination.

L'Embuscade
47, rue de la Rochefoucauld, 75009 Paris
Bar/Restaurant

✳ PROUST'S MADELEINE

For the remembrance of things past: turn back time to your childhood and discover the best cakes and tarts in Paris. Sweet or savory.

Tarterie Les Petits Mitrons
26, rue Lepic, 75018 Paris
Pastry Shop

✳ VINTAGE SUNDAY IN SAINT-OUEN

After searching for vintage stuff, from clothes to old records and furniture in the best Parisian flea market, head to this restaurant to enjoy mussels, fries, and live gypsy jazz.

La Chope des Puces
122, rue des Rosiers, 93400 Saint-Ouen
Flea Market

Acknowledgments

The authors would like to thank Alix Thomsen, who is at the heart of this book.

Thanks to Christian Bragg, Dimitri Coste, Olivier Garros, Johan Lindeberg for BLK DNM, Raphaël Lugassy, Stéphane Manel, Jean-Baptiste Mondino, Sara Nataf, Yarol Poupaud, So-Me, and Annemarieke Van Drimmelen for generously sharing their work with us, as well as Susanna Lea, Shelley Wanger, Naja Baldwin, Françoise Gavalda, and Pei Loi Koay.

Also: Claire Berest, the Berest family, Diene Berete, Bastien Bernini, Fatou Biramah, Paul-Henry Bizon, Odara Carvalho, Carole Chrétiennot (Le Café de Flore), Jeanne Damas, Julien Delajoux, Charlotte Delarue, Emmanuel Delavenne (Hôtel Amour), Emmanuelle Ducournau, Clémentine Goldszal, Camille Gorin, Sébastien Haas, Guillaume Halard, Mark Holgate, Cédric Jimenez, Gina Jimenez, Tina Ka, Nina Klein, Bertrand de Langeron, Magdalena Lawniczak, Pierre Le Ny, Téa and Peter Lundell, Ulrika Lundgren, Saif Mahdhi, the Maigret family, Gaëlle Mancina, Stéphane Manel, Tessa Manel, Jules Mas, Martine Mas, the Mas family, Jean-Philippe Moreaux, Roxana Nadim, Chloé Nataf, Fatou N'Diaye, Anne Sophie Nerrant, Nicolas Nerrant, Next Management Team, Priscille d'Orgeval, Anton Poupaud, Yarol Poupaud, the Poupaud family, Charlotte Poutrelle, Elsa Rakotoson, Gérard Rambert, *Rika* magazine, Joachim Roncin, Christian de Rosnay, Xavier de Rosnay, Martine Saada, Colombe Schneck, Victor Saint Macary, Juliette Seydoux, Sonia Sieff, Samantha Taylor Pickett, Pascal Teixeira, Rodrigo Teixeira, Hervé Temime, Thomsen Paris, Anna Tordjman, Emilie Urbansky, Jean Vedreine (Le Mansart), Camille Vizzavona, Aude Walker, Mathilde Warnier, Adèle Wismes, Rebecca Zlotowski.

Illustration Credits

Audrey, Caroline, Sophie, and Anne

A Note About the Authors

ANNE BEREST is the author of two novels and a biography of Françoise Sagan published this year; she also writes for television, film, and theater.

CAROLINE DE MAIGRET studied literature at the Sorbonne before moving to New York to model. She returned to Paris in 2006 to found her music label. De Maigret has been an ambassador for Chanel since 2012 and supports women worldwide through the NGO CARE.

SOPHIE MAS was born and raised in Paris. After graduating from Sciences Po and HEC, she started her own film company and now works as a producer in Los Angeles, New York, and São Paulo.

AUDREY DIWAN became a scriptwriter after studying journalism and political science. She wrote the screenplay for Cédric Jimenez's *La French,* with Jean Dujardin, and is now directing her first feature film; she is also editor-at-large for the magazine *Stylist.*